COLLINS GEM
ANTIQUES
MARKS

a nine of information

GEM

AID

GW00853303

COLLINS GEM
CRICKET

a nine of information

FAT

a nine of information

DOGS

a nine of information

M

FIRST AID

a nine of information

COLLINS GEM
INTERNET

a nine of information

COLLINS GEM
PREDICTING

a nine of information

COLLINS GEM
Ready
REFERENCE

a nine of information

COLLINS GEM
SHARKS

a nine of information

COLLINS GEM
WHALES
& DOLPHINS

a nine of information

COLLINS GEM
WHISKY

a nine of information

COLLINS GEM
WORD
PROCESSING

a nine of information

COLLINS GEM
Your PC

a nine of information

COLLINS GEM

WORLD
RECORDS

Elaine Henderson

HarperCollins*Publishers*

The author would like to thank the following for their help
and advice in the compilation of this book: Matt Wheeler; Dr
David Henderson; Meteorological Office; Mitchell Library,
Glasgow; National Power; North of Scotland Water
Authority; Wind Energy Group

HarperCollins Publishers
PO Box, Glasgow G4 0NB

First published 1998
This edition published 1999

Reprint 10 9 8 7 6 5 4 3 2 1 0

© HarperCollins Publishers 1999

ISBN 0 00 472293-0

Printed in Italy by Amadeus S.p.A.

Contents

Introduction 5

Earth 7

Space 36

Natural World 49

Precious Stones and Gold 87

Countries of the World 93

Human Life and Society 102

Science and Technology 119

Energy 125

Building and Construction 132

Transport 151

Arts and Entertainment 169

Sport 184

Index 190

Picture Acknowledgments

The publishers would like to acknowledge the following picture libraries for the use of illustrations in this book:

The Bridgeman Art Library

Page 109: *Louis XIV (1638–1715) welcomes the Elector of Saxony, Frederick Augustus I (1750–1827) to Fontainebleau, 1714*, by Louis de Silvestre (1675–1760), Chateau de Versailles, France/Bridgeman Art Library, London/New York

Page 111: *Victoria (1819–1901): from The Times 1897, Diamond Jubilee Presentation*, Guildhall Library, Corporation of London/Bridgeman Art Library, London/New York

Page 117: *Portrait of William Pitt the Younger (1759–1806), c.1782*, by Gainsborough Dupont (1754–97), Private Collection/Bridgeman Art Library, London/New York

Frank Lane Picture Agency

Pages 52, 53, 57, 59, 63, 67, 70, 74

Mary Evans Picture Library

Pages 9, 14, 16–17, 31, 32, 130, 134, 137, 140–41, 152, 173, 179, 182

Hulton Getty Picture Library

Pages 7, 42, 45, 46, 88, 103, 143, 146–47, 154, 158, 165, 176, 185, 189

Introduction

S ome are born record breakers, some set out
to become record breakers and some make
the record books whether they intend to or
not! If you're born a cheetah you're automatically
the fastest sprinter in the world, and if, like Andy
Green, you succeed in breaking the world land
speed record then (at least for the time being!)
you're assured of membership of that most
exclusive club, the world record-holders. And
again, there are people whose passionate devotion
to their work and faith in themselves resulted in
some of the most important scientific,
technological and medical discoveries without
which our modern world would be inconceivable.

In this little book we bring together over 300
different records from across the range of
national and international attributes, feats,
endeavours and achievements, collected under
the broad headings of Natural World, Space,
Science and Technology, Building and
Construction, Sport, Arts and Entertainment, and
so on. Here you can find the oldest living tree in

the world, the coldest planet, the bestselling book and where to find the longest bridge.

To the best of our knowledge all information is correct at the time of going to press but such is the astonishing speed of contemporary progress and scientific discovery, that new records are being set almost daily. We know more about our world today than ever before, but such is the human capacity for curiosity and the world's equally inexhaustible ability to surprise us, that the definitive list of 'world records' may never be compiled!

EARTH

HIGHEST MOUNTAIN
Mt Everest, Tibet/Nepal
29,028 ft (8848 m)

Everest lies in the Himalayan range on the
Tibet/Nepal border (Tibet is now also known by
the Chinese as Xizang). Its Tibetan name,

*Edmund Hillary (with ice axe), Sherpa Tensing (centre) and
expedition leader Colonel John Hunt (left) arrive back in London
having conquered Mt Everest, the world's highest mountain, in
1953*

Chomdungma, translates as 'mother goddess of the world'. The mountain was not scaled until 1953, when two members of a British expedition, the New Zealander Edmund Hillary and Sherpa Tensing Norgay, reached the top.

HIGHEST MOUNTAIN IN EUROPE
Mont Blanc, French/Italian border
15,771 ft (4807 m)
Mont Blanc ('White Mountain') is in the Alps, with its peak in French territory. The Mont Blanc tunnel, bored through the mountain, was opened in 1962; it is $7^1/_4$ miles (11.7 km) long.

HIGHEST MOUNTAIN IN THE UK
Ben Nevis, Scotland
4406 ft (1343 m)
Ben Nevis lies near Fort William in the Highlands of Scotland. Parts of the mountain are covered with snow all year.

HIGHEST MOUNTAIN IN NORTH AMERICA
Mt McKinley, Alaska, USA
20,320 ft (6194 m)
Mt McKinley lies in the Denali National Park;

Ben Nevis, the United Kingdom's highest mountain, overlooks Fort William at the head of Loch Linnhe. This view, taken from a guide to the Caledonian Canal published in the 1870s, shows the mountain from Banavie on the other side of the loch

Denali is the original Athapascan Indian name for the mountain and means 'The Great One'.

HIGHEST MOUNTAIN IN SOUTH AMERICA
Aconcagua, Argentina
22,834 ft (6960 m)

Aconcagua lies in the northern Andes mountains, with its peak in Argentinian territory. It is of volcanic origin, but is not itself a volcano.

HIGHEST MOUNTAIN IN AFRICA
Kilimanjaro, Tanzania
19,340 ft (5895 m)
Kilimanjaro is an extinct volcano and snow-capped all year although, astonishingly, it is only 200 miles (320 km) from the equator.

HIGHEST MOUNTAIN IN ASIA
Mt Everest, Tibet/Nepal
29,028 ft (8848 m)
See HIGHEST MOUNTAIN, *page 7*.

HIGHEST MOUNTAIN IN AUSTRALASIA
Mt Cook, New Zealand
12,349 ft (3764 m)
Mt Cook lies in New Zealand's South Island and is permanently snow-clad.

TALLEST VOLCANIC PEAKS
Hawaiian Islands
29,500 ft (9000 m) from the seabed to the peak
The Hawaiian Islands are formed from the peaks

of huge lava piles which rise from the Pacific Ocean floor to above sea level.

HIGHEST SEA CLIFFS
Hawaii
3314 ft (1010 m)

LONGEST CAVE
Mammoth Cave, Kentucky, USA
329 miles (530 km)
Mammoth Cave has many interconnecting passages and spreads over five different levels. The flow of the Echo river which runs through it continues to wear away the rock and make the cave system even larger. The river is the habitat of a species of blind fish, *Amblyopsis spelaea*, found nowhere else in the world.

LONGEST CAVE IN THE UK
Ease Gill, England
32 1/2 miles (52.5 km) explored length

DEEPEST CAVE
Jean Bernard, France
5036 ft (1535 m)

DEEPEST CAVE IN THE UK
Ffynnon Dhu, Wales
1010 ft (308 m)

LARGEST CAVE
Sarawak Chamber, Sarawak, Malaysia
2297 ft (700 m) long, 1312 ft (400 m) wide, 230 ft (70 m) high

LONGEST STALACTITE
Poll an Ionana, Republic of Ireland
20 ft 6 in (6.2 m) long
Stalactites and stalagmites are formed from calcium carbonate precipitated out of water that trickles from the roof of a cave. Stalactites grow downwards from the roof.

TALLEST STALAGMITE
Krásnohorská Cave, Czech Republic
105 ft (32 m)
Stalagmites grow upwards from the cave floor and can reach greater lengths than the more fragile stalactites.

LARGEST SALTWATER LAKE
Caspian Sea, Azerbaijan/Iran/Kazakhstan/Russia

149,200 miles² (386,400 km²)

The surface of the Caspian Sea is now 92 ft (28 m) below world sea level. The sea is fed by the Volga river (the longest in Europe, *see page 18*) and is tideless. In some places the Caspian Sea reaches depths of some 2500 ft (750 m).

LARGEST NATURAL FRESHWATER LAKE

Lake Superior, Canada/USA
31,700 miles² (82,100 km²)

Lake Superior is one of the five Great Lakes which border Canada and the USA and, together, cover the same area as the entire United Kingdom. Lake Superior lies about 600 ft (180 m) above sea level and has an average depth of some 475 ft (145 m).

LARGEST NATURAL FRESHWATER LAKE IN THE UK (AREA)

Loch Lomond, Scotland
120 miles² (312 km²)

Loch Lomond lies northwest of Glasgow and is one of Scotland's most picturesque lochs.

A 1930s postcard from Loch Ness, a double record-holder in the United Kingdom, showing 'The haunts of the monster'

LARGEST NATURAL FRESHWATER LAKE IN THE UK (VOLUME)

Loch Ness, Scotland

23 miles (36 km) long, 788 ft (240 m) deep

Loch Ness lies in the Great Glen, the rift that bisects the Highlands of Scotland. It is fed by several rivers and flows out via the River Ness to the Moray Firth. The 'Loch Ness Monster' stories date back to the seventh century, although long-held beliefs that the loch is bottomless have been proved to be unfounded.

DEEPEST NATURAL FRESHWATER LAKE
Lake Baikal, Russia
Up to 5000 ft (1525 m)

Lake Baikal contains about one fifth of the earth's fresh water.

DEEPEST NATURAL FRESHWATER LAKE IN THE UK
Loch Ness, Scotland
788 ft (240 m) deep

See LARGEST NATURAL FRESHWATER LAKE IN THE UK (VOLUME), *page 14.*

LONGEST GORGE
Grand Canyon, USA
280 miles (450 km)

The Grand Canyon, Arizona, was formed by the Colorado river which runs through it. Over billions of years the river has cut through the rock to a depth of 5900 ft (1800 m), exposing many different layers of rock and giving a complete geological history of the area. The rocks at the base of the canyon are older than 570 million years, formed in the time when the only living creatures were single-celled organisms in the oceans.

The Grand Canyon is the longest gorge in the world, at 280 miles (450 km). This painting by an unnamed artist originally appeared in The Inland Printer *of April 1905*

LONGEST RIVER
Nile
4132 miles (6650 km)
The Nile flows through Tanzania, Uganda, Sudan and Egypt from its source in the mountains of Burundi to the delta on the Mediterranean coast.

LONGEST RIVER IN EUROPE
Volga
2193 miles (3529 km)
The Volga rises in the Valdai Hills, northwest of Moscow, and flows into the Caspian Sea (*see* **LARGEST SALTWATER LAKE**, *page 12*). The river basin occupies some 533,000 miles^2 (1,380,000 km^2).

LONGEST RIVER IN THE UK
Severn
200 miles (322 km)
The Severn rises near the River Wye and flows out to the Bristol Channel and the Atlantic Ocean. The Severn estuary is noted for its tidal bore – a wave up to 3 ft (1 m) high caused by the incoming tide.

LONGEST RIVER IN NORTH AMERICA
Mackenzie-Peace

2635 miles (4241 km) total length

The Mackenzie rises from the Great Slave Lake in the Canadian Northwest Territories and flows northward to the Beaufort Sea of the Arctic Ocean. The Finlay river, its farthest headstream, flows into the Peace River Reservoir.

LONGEST RIVER IN SOUTH AMERICA
Amazon

4000 miles (6437 km)

The Amazon rises in the Peruvian Andes and flows through northern Brazil to the Atlantic Ocean. It has more than 1000 tributaries and it is estimated that 20 per cent of all the water that runs off the surface of the earth becomes part of the river.

LONGEST RIVER IN AFRICA
Nile

4132 miles (6650 km)

See **LONGEST RIVER**, *page 18.*

LONGEST RIVER IN ASIA
Yangtze

3400 miles (5472 km)

Also known as Ch'ang Chiang or Chang Jiang, the Yangtze rises on the Plateau of Tibet in western China, and flows through 12 Chinese provinces and regions before it reaches its delta on the East China Sea.

LONGEST RIVER IN AUSTRALASIA
Murray
1609 miles (2589 km)
The Australian Murray river lies between New South Wales and Victoria; it flows through the Snowy Mountains to the Indian Ocean.

HIGHEST WATERFALL
Angel Falls (Salto Angelo), Venezuela
3212 ft (979 m) total height, 2560 ft (780 m) highest uninterrupted drop
The Angel Falls (Churún Merú to the Indians) were named after the American pilot, Jimmy Angel, who first recorded them as he flew over the top in 1933.

HIGHEST WATERFALL IN EUROPE
Utigardsfossen Falls, Norway
2625 ft (800 m)
The water in the Utigardsfossen Falls comes from

the Josterdal Glacier. Waterfalls are created when rivers flow for thousands of years over bands of hard and soft rock. The river wears away the softer rock downstream more quickly and where the different types of rock meet, the river will plunge over the resulting edge of harder rock. In terms of the geological timescale, waterfalls are temporary features of the landscape.

LARGEST WATERFALL (BY VOLUME)
Chutes de Khone (Khone Falls),
Kampuchea/Laos
230 ft (70 m) high, 2,500,000 gallons (9,500,000 litres) per second, estimated flow

LARGEST GLACIER
Lambert Glacier, Antarctica
250 miles (402 km)
Glaciers are sheets of ice, formed when the winter snowfall exceeds the summer melt. The snow is compressed and is gradually transformed into ice. Each year the same process allows the ice mass to grow and it also becomes tougher and harder. Most, but not all, glaciers move.

FASTEST-MOVING GLACIER
Rinks Isbrae, Greenland
90 ft (28 m) per day

Glaciers usually move quite slowly, but they may occasionally have surges of speed. In 1963/4, for example, Brúarjökull Glacier in Iceland moved 410 ft (125 m) per day for over two months.

LARGEST DESERT
Sahara, Africa
3,320,000 miles² (8,600,000 km²)

The Sahara occupies one quarter of the African continent and stretches from the Atlantic Ocean to the Red Sea, bordering 11 countries. Its name means 'wilderness' in Arabic. Rock paintings, some 6000 years old, have been discovered in the Sahara, showing that it was once a fertile place, home to elephants and cattle.

LARGEST OCEAN
Pacific Ocean
Up to 10,700 miles (18,115 km) at greatest width

The Pacific is twice the size of the Atlantic Ocean and has a greater area than all the land surfaces of the world put together. The ocean stretches from the Bering Straits on the Arctic Circle to Cape

Adare, Antarctica. It is probably the world's oldest ocean, estimated to be some 600 million years old.

DEEPEST OCEAN
Pacific Ocean
Mean depth 14,040 ft (4280 m), greatest depth 36,200 ft (11,034 m)

The deepest point of the Pacific so far discovered is the Mariana Trench, a depression in the ocean floor near the Mariana Islands. In 1960, Jacques Picard recorded the deepest-ever dive, in his father's bathyscaphe *Trieste*, by going as far as 35,800 ft (10,911 m) into the trench.

LARGEST SEA
Arabian Sea
1,491,000 miles² (3,862,000 km²)

The Arabian Sea forms the northwest section of the Indian Ocean, bounded by India, Pakistan, Iran, the Arabian Peninsula and the Horn of Africa. Depths exceed 9800 ft (2987 m).

HIGHEST WAVE
110 ft (34 m) estimated

This wave was reported by the United States ship

Ramapoo during bad weather in the North Pacific in 1933. 'Freak waves' are caused by the collision of two sets of waves travelling in opposite directions. The highest such wave instrumentally recorded was 85 ft (26 m) by the British ship *Weather Reporter* in the North Atlantic in December 1972.

HIGHEST TSUNAMI
1000 ft (304 m)

Tsunamis are also called tidal waves, although they have nothing to do with tides. They are, in fact, usually caused by earthquakes, especially those that disturb the ocean floor. Tsunamis can travel long distances at enormous speeds (up to 500 mph (805 km/h) and pose no threat in open seas, rising only to about 3 ft (1 m) high. However, as they slow down in shallow waters they suddenly surge to enormous heights – some have even been known to lift up entire ships. They then crash down on the land, destroying everything in their path.

LARGEST ISLAND
Greenland
840,000 miles² (2,175,600 km²)

Greenland, a self-governing Danish dependency,

lies in the north Atlantic Ocean, with two-thirds of the island within the Arctic Circle. Greenland's principal feature is its massive ice sheet, second only to that of Antarctica in size, which extends for over 700,000 miles^2 (1,813,000 km^2), almost 85 per cent of the country's total land mass. The capital is Nuuk, the only sizeable town, and the entire population numbers just 56,000.

HIGHEST TEMPERATURE RECORDED
136 °F (57.8 °C)
Al' Azízíah, Libya, 13 September 1922 and San Louis, Mexico, 11 August 1933

HIGHEST TEMPERATURE RECORDED IN THE UK
98.8 °F (37.1 °C)
Cheltenham, Gloucestershire, England, 3 August 1990

LOWEST TEMPERATURE RECORDED
–128.56 °F (– 89.2 °C)
Vostok Base, Antarctica, 21 July 1983

LOWEST TEMPERATURE RECORDED IN THE UK
–17 °F (–27.2 °C)

Braemar, Scotland, 11 February 1895 and
10 January 1982

HOTTEST INHABITED PLACE
Dalol, Ethiopia
Average annual temperature 94 °F (34.4 °C)

HIGHEST ANNUAL RAINFALL
905.12 in (22,990 mm)
Cherrapunji, India, 1861

GREATEST RAINFALL IN ONE CALENDAR MONTH
366.14 in (9150 mm)
Cherrapunji, India, July 1861

GREATEST RAINFALL IN ONE DAY
73.62 in (1840 mm)
Cilaos, Isle de Réunion, 16 March 1952

GREATEST RAINFALL IN ONE MINUTE
1.23 in (30 mm)
Unionville, Maryland, USA

HIGHEST ANNUAL RAINFALL IN THE UK
257 in (6430 mm)

Sprinkling Tarn, Cumbria, 1954

GREATEST RAINFALL IN ONE DAY IN THE UK
11 in (280 mm)
Martinstown, Dorset, 18 July 1955

LOWEST ANNUAL RAINFALL
0.03 in (0.008 mm)
Arica, Chile

DRIEST PLACE (LONGEST DROUGHT)
Atacama Desert, Chile
The Atacama Desert forms part of the Atacama region of Chile, bounded on the east by Argentina and on the west by the Pacific Ocean. The desert is about 600–700 miles (966–1126 km) long. Some meteorological stations in the area have never recorded any rain at all, although heavy rains are known to fall in the desert between two and four times each century.

LARGEST CLOUDS
Cumulonimbus
Up to 6 miles (9.7 km) high
Clouds of this magnitude would contain up to half a million tons (508,000 tonnes) of water.

HIGHEST RECORDED WIND SPEED
231 mph (371 km/h)
Mt Washington Observatory, New Hampshire, USA, 12 April 1934

FASTEST GUST OF WIND IN THE UK
153 mph (246 km/h)
Cairngorm, Scotland, 20 March 1986

FASTEST WINDS ON EARTH
Up to 300 mph (483 km/h)
Winds of these speeds are found inside the funnels of tornados.

HEAVIEST HAILSTONES
2.20 lb (1 kg)
Gopalganj, Bangladesh, 1986
Over 90 people were killed in this hailstorm, which also caused considerable damage to property. Hailstones are formed in thunderclouds: the air currents push water droplets upwards to the top of the cloud, where they freeze in the cold air. The droplets then fall down, accumulating additional layers of freezing water as they go. Currents may then force them up again to the top of the cloud,

where they harden further before falling again, and this process can be repeated several times until the hailstone finally falls to earth. The largest recorded hailstone in the UK weighed 5.25 oz (150 g).

LARGEST PIECE OF ICE TO FALL TO EARTH
20 ft (6 m) diameter
Ord, Scotland, 13 August 1849

LARGEST RECORDED SNOWFLAKE
15 in x 8 in (38 cm x 20 cm)
Fort Keogh, Montana, USA, 28 January 1887

MOST POWERFUL VOLCANIC ERUPTION
Krakatoa, Indonesia, 26/27 August 1883
Krakatoa is a small, mountainous island in the Sunda Strait, between Sumatra and Java, Indonesia. The volcano was generally considered to be safe and no one could have foreseen the events that began at 1 pm on 26 August 1883 when the island began to blow up and disintegrate. Explosions were heard in Australia, some 2000 miles (3219 km) away; ash was sent 50 miles (80 km) up into the air. Sulphurous winds blew across the water, and strange glowing electrical discharges

flickered round the masts of ships, known as St Elmo's Fire. The air for miles was choked with burning ash, supercharged with static electricity and huge lightning bolts terrified sailors at sea. Tsunamis (*see* **HIGHEST TSUNAMI**, *page 24*) struck Java and other islands, causing death and destruction, and darkness fell for days over the whole region. Dust in the upper atmosphere blocked sunlight, causing a worldwide drop in air temperature over a number of years.

WORST VOLCANIC ERUPTION IN THE 20TH CENTURY
Mt Pelée, Martinique, 5/8 May 1902

Martinique, in the West Indies, was a French colony in 1902. Its main crop was sugar and the principal town, St Pierre, a picturesque place only 6 miles (10 km) from the volcano. At 7.50 am on 8 May, the explosions began, followed by an avalanche of burning gas and ash, known as a *nuée ardente* (glowing cloud), surging towards St Pierre, and moving at around 115 mph (185 km/h). Over 30,000 people died. Only two are known to have survived; one, ironically a convicted murderer, was imprisoned in a windowless cell and escaped with severe burns.

When Krakatoa erupted in 1883, huge amounts of ash were catapulted into the air and upper atmosphere. This illustration by F.H. Schell from the Cosmopolitan Magazine *of 1894 gives some idea of the conditions endured by vessels in the area*

A spectacular painting of Mt Etna, the highest active volcano in Europe, completed in 1869 by Eugène Ciceri

HIGHEST ACTIVE VOLCANO
19,876 ft (6060 m)
Cotopaxi, Ecuador

HIGHEST ACTIVE VOLCANO IN EUROPE
10,899 ft (3323 m)
Mt Etna, Sicily, Italy

TALLEST GEYSER
195–380 ft (60–115 m)

Yellowstone National Park, Wyoming, USA
Geysers are found in volcanic regions in the USA, Iceland and New Zealand and are produced when underground water is in contact with hot rock. Water under pressure in part of an irregularly shaped geyser tube may reach a temperature higher than boiling point, producing steam which rises up through the tube and forces out the water above it. There are over 3000 geysers and hot springs in Yellowstone.

WORST EARTHQUAKE
Upper Egypt/Syria, 1201
Over one million people are thought to have died in this earthquake, estimated at IX on the Mercalli Scale*. Earthquakes are explained by plate tectonics: the earth's crust is composed of large, rigid plates that move; where two plates converge, known as a fault line, severe pressures are built up, until the stress is so great that the rocks split and shift.

* Mercalli Scale – the 12 degrees of intensity (I–XII) indicate the amount of damage caused: XII = total destruction.

WORST EARTHQUAKE IN THE 20TH CENTURY
Tangshan, China, 28 July 1976

It is estimated that around 250,000 people died during the earthquake and its aftershocks. The Tangshan earthquake was judged to be XI on the Mercalli Scale* and 7.8 on the Richter Scale.**

MOST POWERFUL EARTHQUAKE RECORDED INSTRUMENTALLY
8.5 Richter Scale**
Southern Chile, 22 May 1960

The earthquake covered a subterranean area of some 620 miles (1000 km) long by 180 miles (290 km) wide. There were a large number of shocks and aftershocks over a wide area.

---

* Mercalli Scale – the 12 degrees of intensity (I–XII) indicate the amount of damage caused: XII = total destruction.

** Richter Scale – indicates the amount of energy released by the earthquake. There is no upper limit.

MOST POWERFUL RECORDED EARTHQUAKE IN THE UK
5.4 Richter Scale**
North Wales, July 1984

MOST POWERFUL HURRICANE RECORDED INSTRUMENTALLY
Level 5: Catastrophic
Hurricane Andrew, August 1992
Hurricane Andrew was rated 5 (the top level) on the international scale; this is reserved for hurricanes with winds of 155 mph (250 km/h) and storm surges of over 18 ft (5.5 m).

SPACE

LARGEST PLANET
Jupiter
85,680 miles (142,800 km) diameter

Jupiter is named after the Roman king of the gods
and ruler of the universe. It is composed mainly of
hydrogen and helium and its core is thought to be
hotter than that of the sun itself, with an estimated
temperature of some 5400 °F (3000 °C). Jupiter
has 16 known moons.

SMALLEST PLANET
Pluto
1430 miles (2302 km) diameter

Named after the Roman god who ruled over the
dead in the Underworld, Pluto is a frozen, lifeless
world with an estimated temperature of −382 °F
(−230 °C), thus making it the coldest of the planets.
It has one moon.

NEAREST PLANET
Venus
25,000,000 miles (41,000,000 km) estimated
distance from earth

The brightest object in the sky, after the sun and moon, Venus is named after the Roman goddess of love. Its atmosphere is made up mainly of carbon dioxide, and it is the hottest planet with an estimated surface temperature of 842–896 °F (450–480 °C).

FURTHEST PLANET VISIBLE TO THE NAKED EYE
Uranus
1,687,000,000 miles (2,720,000,000 km) estimated distance from earth
Uranus is named after the Greek god of the sky. Its atmosphere is composed of hydrogen, helium and methane, approximately 6000 miles (10,000 km) thick, and it is surrounded by a system of narrow rings, thought to contain rock fragments and ice. Uranus is only marginally less cold than Pluto, with temperatures around −354 °F (−220 °C).

FURTHEST PLANET
Pluto
3,567,000,000 miles (5,750,000,000 km) estimated distance from earth
See SMALLEST PLANET, *page 36.*

LARGEST STAR
Σ Aurigae
2,336,000,000 miles (3759,000,000 km) diameter estimated

Σ Aurigae is the largest known star to date. A white supergiant, it lies in the constellation of Auriga and is about 2000 light years* away from earth.

SMALLEST STAR
Neutron stars (pulsars)
12–19 miles (20–30 km) diameter

Pulsars are tiny, highly-condensed neutron stars which spin at extremely high speeds, and have a very high density of up to 8000 million tons per in³ (500 million tonnes per cm³).

CLOSEST STAR
Alpha Centauri
4.35 light years* from Earth

Alpha Centauri is a red dwarf, lying in the Centaurus constellation in the Milky Way.

---

*One light year = 5,874,000,000,000 miles (9,453,000,000,000 km). This is the distance that light travels in one year.

BRIGHTEST STAR
Sirius
8.64 light years* from earth
Sirius, also known as the Dog Star, is a binary star in the constellation of Canis Major.

LARGEST ASTEROID
Ceres
623 miles (1003 km) diameter
Asteroids, also known as minor planets and planetoids, are the small, celestial bodies which move around the sun, mainly between the orbits of Mars and Jupiter (the Asteroid Belt). They appear as tiny points of light in powerful telescopes. Ceres was discovered in 1801 by Giuseppe Piazzi, Professor of Theology and Mathematics at Palermo University, and was named after the Roman goddess of agriculture and patron goddess of Sicily. Asteroids of varying sizes frequently fall to earth, causing various degrees of damage.

FIRST REFLECTING TELESCOPE (REFLECTOR)
1668
Invented by Isaac Newton, the reflector works by collecting and focusing light by reflection from a

curved mirror (*compare* REFRACTOR, *below*). Light of all colours is reflected in the same way, thus eliminating the blurring and fringing which characterized the early refracting telescopes, such as that used by Galileo. Large mirrors can be constructed more easily than large lenses, can be made more accurate, and can be positioned more easily.

LARGEST REFLECTOR IN THE WORLD
32 ft 9 in (10 m)
Keck telescope, Mauna Kea Observatory, Hawaii, USA

This multi-mirror telescope was completed in 1992 and is used for optical and infra-red observations.

LARGEST REFRACTING TELESCOPE (REFRACTOR)
40 in (102 cm) lens diameter
Yerkes Observatory, Williams Bay, Wisconsin, USA

The refractor works by using a large lens (the objective) to gather light rays from a distant source and, by refraction, bending them to a focal point. The observer then looks at a magnified image. The main problems include blurring and colour fringing because different colours of light refract by different amounts (e.g. blue light bends more than red). No one knows who invented the first refractor, although it may have been Hans Lippershey, a Dutch spectacle-maker, in around 1608.

FIRST RADIO TELESCOPE
Circa 1940
USA, invented by Grote Reber
The principles are similar to those of the optical reflecting telescope: a thin sheet of metal covers a very large parabolic surface that focuses radiation onto a small antenna connected to a sensitive radio receiver.

LARGEST FULLY-STEERABLE DISH RADIO TELESCOPE
250 ft (76 m)
Jodrell Bank Experimental Station, Cheshire, England
The radio telescope at Jodrell Bank was begun in 1952 and completed in 1957, just before the launch of *Sputnik I*, the first artificial earth satellite. The

The 250 ft (76 m) dish of the world's largest fully-steerable dish radio telescope can clearly be seen in this aerial photograph of the Jodrell Bank Experimental Station

satellite's carrier rocket was tracked at Jodrell Bank
by radar and the installation transmitted the first
pictures of the moon's surface sent by the Soviet
Luna probe on 6 February 1966.

LARGEST SINGLE-UNIT RADIO TELESCOPE
1000 ft (305 m) diameter antenna
Arecibo, Puerto Rico, USA

The installation lies in a hollow high in the mountains.

LARGEST RADIO INTERFEROMETER (ARRAY)
VLA (Very Large Array), Socorro, New Mexico, USA

An interferometer or array works by linking two or
more dishes together electronically, thereby
effectively making one enormous instrument and
greatly increasing capacity. The VLA was
completed in 1979 and is laid out in a Y-shape with
arms 13 miles (21 km) long. Each arm is a railway,
thus allowing the 27 separate telescopes, each with
a diameter of 81 feet (25 m), to be moved
according to need. The installation gives a very
high resolution image of cosmic radio sources and
is the largest astronomical instrument ever built; it
cost over $100 million.

LARGEST SPACE TELESCOPE
Hubble Space Telescope (HST)

The Hubble Space Telescope is a large reflector with a 7 ft 10 in (2.4 m) primary mirror, a secondary mirror and state-of-the-art instruments that can detect visible, ultraviolet and infra-red light. The telescope was put into orbit on 25 April 1990 about 370 miles (600 km) above the earth by the crew of the space shuttle *Discovery*. Unfortunately there were problems with the reflecting mirror and it became the first satellite to be repaired in space.

FIRST SPACE PROBE TO LEAVE THE SOLAR SYSTEM
Pioneer 10

Unmanned space probes are used for interplanetary study. *Pioneer 10* (launched 1972) was designed to fly past Jupiter and continue out into deep space. In 1987 it became the first manmade object to leave the solar system, and is now billions of miles away and still travelling. It carries a plaque giving details about the earth and its origins.

FIRST MAN IN SPACE
Yuri Alexeyevich Gargarin, USSR

Yuri Gargarin (1934-68) volunteered for space

On 12 April 1961 the Russian Yuri Gargarin became the first man in space

On 20 July 1969 the American Neil Armstrong became the first man to walk on the moon

training and was launched on 12 April 1961 in *Vostok I*. The duration of the flight was 1 hr 48 min and he travelled some 25,000 miles (40,232 km) at altitudes of between 112 miles (180 km) and 203 miles (327 km) at a speed of approximately 5 miles (8 km) per second. A national hero, Cosmonaut Gargarin was killed in a plane crash while training for another mission.

FIRST WOMAN IN SPACE
Valentina Vladimirovna Tereshkova, USSR

On 16 June 1963, Tereshkova (born 1937) was launched into space on the *Vostok 6*. She circled the earth 48 times in 70 hr 50 min, travelling a distance of some 1,225,000 miles (1,971,000 km).

FIRST MAN ON THE MOON
Neil A. Armstrong, USA

Neil Armstrong (born 1930), Edward 'Buzz' Aldrin and Michael Collins landed the *Apollo 11* in the Sea of Tranquillity on the moon on 20 July 1969. Armstrong's moon walk was an event unparalleled in human history and his words 'The Eagle has landed' and 'That's one small step for [a] man, one giant leap for mankind' were heard by an estimated

600 million people, about one-fifth of the entire
world population.

FIRST BRITON IN SPACE
Helen Sharman

Sharman, a British chemist, won a competition to
travel as a guest on the Russian *Mir* space station.
She flew to *Mir* on the *Soyuz TM12* craft on 18
May 1991 and returned on 26 May.

LONGEST SPACE FLIGHT FOR A MAN
439 days
Valery Polyakov, Russia

Polyakov travelled to the *Mir* space station on
Soyuz TM18 in January 1994 and returned on
Soyuz TM20 in March 1995. Polyakov has a career
total of 680 days in space.

LONGEST SPACE FLIGHT FOR A WOMAN
174 days
Yelena Kondakova, Russia

Kondakova landed back on earth on 22 March
1995 after 174 days on the *Mir* space station.

NATURAL WORLD

TALLEST TREE
Coast redwood (*Sequoia sempervirens*)
Max height circa 400 ft (120 m)
Max diameter of trunk 30 ft (10 m)
The coast redwood is an evergreen tree, native only
to the Pacific coast of North America (the 'fog
belt'), up to some 3300 ft (1000 m) above sea level.

TALLEST NATIVE EUROPEAN TREE
Common silver fir (*Abies alba*)
Approx 165–245 ft (50–75 m) high
The silver fir is native to the mountainous regions
of central and southern Europe. However, its
attractive, lofty stature has made it a popular
ornamental tree throughout Europe and it is often
found in parks and gardens.

LARGEST TREE (GIRTH)
Giant redwood or giant sequoia, also called
sierra redwood, big tree, mammoth tree,
wellingtonia (*Sequoiadendron giganteum*)
Max 101 ft 6 in (31 m) circumference at base
The largest-known specimen, the General Sherman

Tree, is in the Sequoia National Park in the USA. It stands approximately 272 ft (83 m) tall and is estimated to weigh over 6000 tons (6096 tonnes). The trees are native to the western slopes of the Sierra Nevada mountain range in California, and can grow at an altitude of up to 8000 ft (2500 m).

LONGEST-LIVED TREE
Bristlecone pine (*Pinus aristata* or *Pinus longaeva*)
Circa 5000 years
The Bristlecone pine is a native of the Rocky Mountains in the south-west of North America. It grows extremely slowly in the high altitude conditions, usually over an altitude of 7500 ft (2300 m).

OLDEST KNOWN SURVIVING SPECIES OF TREE
Maidenhair tree (*Ginkgo biloba*)
The maidenhair dates from the Mesozoic era, especially the Jurassic period, approximately 160 million years ago, the age of the dinosaurs.

LARGEST SEED
Sea coconut or coco de mer (*Lodoicea maldivica*)
30–40 lb (13–18 kg)
The sea coconut tree is today found on only two
islands in the Seychelles, Praslin and Curiense;
there are only about 4000 trees left and they are
strictly protected. The tree grows to about 100-140
ft (30-40 m), has a lovely, fan-shaped canopy and
lives up to about 800 years.

SMALLEST SEEDS
Orchids, such as the tiny, almost microscopic
Platystele stenostachya, one of the world's smallest
flowering plants, produce microscopic seeds.
These orchids are native to Central America and
the northern parts of South America.

LARGEST POD
Entada scandens
Approx 5 ft (1.5 m) long
The *Entada* grows in tropical forests and is a woody
climber. The pod, though long, is only about 4 in
(10 cm) wide; it holds up to 15 seeds and hangs
down from the stem (this plant also has one of the
longest-known plant stems, up to 460 ft (140 m)).

PLANT WITH THE MOST MASSIVE LEAVES
Gigantic waterlily (*Victoria amazonica*)
Up to 6 ft (2 m) diameter
The huge, flat leaves are turned up at the edges,
like a tray, and can support the weight of a child.

The gigantic waterlily has leaves up to 6 ft (2 m) in diameter

SMALLEST PLANT
Watermeal (*Wolffia arrhiza*)
0.08 in (2 mm) wide
Wolffia is an angiosperm, or flowering plant.
Angiosperms are the largest and most diverse

group in the plant kingdom and represent approximately 80 per cent of all known green plants now living. This tiny, floating herb is scarcely visible to the naked eye.

LARGEST FLOWER
Rafflesia (*Rafflesia arnoldii*)
Approx 3 ft 4 in (1 m) diameter, up to 15$\frac{1}{2}$ lb (7 kg) weight

The gigantic bloom is brownish-red with white patches and resembles rotting meat, both in shape and smell, an attribute that evolved to attract the

Rafflesia may well have the world's largest flower but the tropical heat of Sumatra and Borneo where it grows means that each flower only lasts for four days

insects which are necessary for pollination. The bloom is short-lived; after four days it quickly disintegrates in the tropical heat. *Rafflesia* is found in tropical forests in Sumatra and Borneo; it grows as a parasite on the roots of other plants and has neither stalk nor leaves.

LARGEST CACTUS
Saguaro (*Carnegia gigantea*)
Up to 53 ft (16 m) height, up to 10 tons (10,000 kg) weight

The saguaro is a native of the Sonora Desert, Mexico, and south-west California. It is a striking plant, its thick arms emerging from the stem at the same height on each side, and turning upwards, resembling a candelabra. It can store up to 5300 pints (3000 litres) of water and lives up to 200 years.

LARGEST MUSHROOM
Puffball (*Calvatia gigantea*)
Up to 5 ft (1.55 m) diameter

This huge specimen was found in the USA, but puffballs are generally much smaller, averaging around 9 in–1 ft (20–30 cm) in diameter. A puffball

contains around three trillion spores which it sheds
when it bursts.

MOST POISONOUS MUSHROOM
Death cap (*Amanita phalloides*)
Mortality rate 60–100 per cent
Death cap can easily be mistaken for an edible
mushroom of similar appearance and does not
taste bad. Symptoms only appear 9–14 hours
after eating, by which time it is usually too late.
The chemicals in death cap dissolve blood
corpuscles.

LARGEST MAMMAL
Blue whale (*Balaenoptera musculus*)
**80–90 ft (24–27 m) long, 128–148 tons (130–150
tonnes) weight**
Blue whales are a dark, blue-grey colour with paler
markings, and usually travel alone or in pairs,
rarely in schools. They live in deep waters both
north and south of the equator and feed on krill
(tiny, shrimp-like creatures). Intensive whaling in
the past decimated the whale numbers and very
large specimens are rarely seen today.

LARGEST LAND MAMMAL
African elephant (*Loxodonta africana africana*)
Approx 10 ft (3 m) height, 6 tons (6.096 tonnes)
weight, 27 ft (9 m) long (male)
African elephants rarely grow to heights of more
than 11 ft (3.5 m), although a specimen was found
to be 12 ft (3.6 m) at the shoulder. Elephants are
herbivores and their weight varies according to the
season and what vegetation is available.

HEAVIEST LAND MAMMAL
See **LARGEST LAND MAMMAL** *above.*

TALLEST MAMMAL
Giraffe (*Giraffa camelopardalis*)
18 ft (5.5 m) average height (male)
The giraffe is found only in Africa today, living in
the dry lands and open wooded areas south of the
Sahara desert. It feeds mainly on leaves and,
because of its elongated neck, is superbly equipped
to reach the topmost branches of the trees.

SMALLEST MAMMAL
Kitti's hog-nosed bat (*Craseonycteris*
thonglongyai*)

The African elephant is the world's largest land mammal, growing to a height of approximately 10 ft (3 m). This male elephant was photographed in the Ngorongoro Crater in Tanzania

6 in (15 cm) wingspan, 1¹/₂ in (4 cm) body length

This tiny creature weighs only 0.42–0.84 oz (1.5–3 g) and is found in small groups in bamboo forests and teak plantations. A nocturnal animal, it is insectivorous and spends the daylight hours roosting in caves. Kitti's hog-nosed bat (also called the butterfly bat) is in serious danger of becoming extinct as the total world population is only about 200 individuals.

FASTEST LAND MAMMAL (SHORT DISTANCES)

Cheetah (*Acinonyx jubatus*)

71 mph (105 km/h) max

Cheetahs live in open grasslands and semi-arid deserts in Africa and south-west Asia. They hunt small-hoofed animals, such as impala and gazelle, which gather in herds out in the open, away from cover. To be successful, therefore, the cheetah needs to be able to attack animals moving at speed away from it. The cheetah can reach 0–50 mph (0–80 km/h) within 2 seconds and a maximum speed of 71 mph (105 km/h). The average chase covers about 600 ft (183 m) and lasts 20 seconds,

before the prey is killed swiftly and cleanly with a
bite through the neck.

FASTEST LAND MAMMAL (LONG DISTANCES)
Pronghorn antelope (*Antilocapra americana*)
45 mph (70 km/h) over 4 miles (6.4 km)

The pronghorn antelope lives in the open grass and
bushlands of the western USA, Canada and parts
of Mexico. It has a heavy, thickset body with long,

*A cheetah can reach speeds of over 70 mph (105 km/h) when
pursuing its prey. This cheetah is about to catch a Thomson's
gazelle and was photographed in the Masai Mara reserve, Kenya*

slim legs. The black horns are shed and regrown
annually. The pronghorn can run as fast as 55 mph
(86 km/h) over short distances as well as maintain a
steady 45 mph (70 km/h) over longer distances.

SLOWEST MAMMAL
Three-toed sloth (*Bradypus tridactylus*)
6–8 ft (1.8–2.5 m) per minute (average ground speed)

The sloth lives in the rainforests of Central and
South America, spending most of its time in the
trees, where it hangs upside down from branches.
Its coat, which is never groomed, often acquires a
greenish colour from the algae growing on it, and
the hair grows in the opposite direction from that
of most animals, i.e. from stomach to back, thereby
preventing waterlogging when the animal is
hanging upside down. The leaf-eating sloth has few
competitors for the food it needs and remains
almost unnoticeable to predators in the dense
forest. However, the continuing survival of this
unique animal depends on humans and their
willingness to protect the remaining tropical
forests.

LONGEST-LIVED MAMMAL (MARINE)

Humpback whale (*Megaptera novaeangliae*)
Fin whale (*Balaenoptera physalus*)

Both species can live up to 95 years.

LONGEST-LIVED MAMMAL (LAND)

Asiatic elephant (*Elephas maximus*)
Up to 60 years (80 in captivity)

MAMMAL WHICH LIVES AT GREATEST ALTITUDE

Mount Everest pika (*Ochotona wollastoni*)
Up to 20,000 ft (6100 m) altitude

Pikas are small, short-eared, tailless herbivores, related to rabbits. They are widespread throughout North America, eastern Europe, the Middle East and parts of Asia. Brownish-grey in colour, the pika grows up to about 8 in (20 cm) long and weighs up to about 10 oz (280 g).

MAMMAL WHICH LIVES AT GREATEST DEPTH

Myotis lucifugus
Up to 3000 ft (915 m) depth

Myotis lucifugus is a species of bat, some of which

inhabit very deep caves and can survive a core
body temperature as low as 23 °F (−5 °C) when
hibernating. There are about 1000 species of bat
worldwide and they are found in most parts of the
world. All bat species found in the UK are now
protected.

DEEPEST-DIVING MAMMAL
Sperm whale (*Physeter catodon*)
Up to 10,000 ft (3050 m) depth

The sperm whale is characterized by a large,
squarish head which makes up a third of its length.

LARGEST PRIMATE
Gorilla (*Gorilla gorilla*)
Up to 6 ft 6 in (2 m) height, 310–400 lb
(140–180 kg) weight (adult male)

The gorilla has a fearsome reputation, perhaps
because of its powerful, muscular body, but in fact
it is a gentle animal, living in close-knit family
groups in the equatorial forests of Africa. Gorillas
are herbivorous and move each day to find fresh
food. They are generally shy animals and will only
become ferocious when provoked. Together with
the chimpanzee, the gorilla is man's closest relative.

The gorilla is the world's largest primate, weighing up to 400 lb (180 kg), yet despite its bulk it is a surprisingly shy animal

SMALLEST PRIMATE
Lesser mouse lemur (*Microcebus myoxinus*)
Up to 4 in (12.5 cm) body length, 5–6 in (13–15 cm) tail length

Lemurs are found only on the island of Madagascar, off the east coast of Africa, and appear to have evolved after the island broke away from the mainland millions of years ago. The lesser mouse lemur has large eyes, a long, bushy tail and slender limbs. Mainly nocturnal and arboreal, this lemur eats insects, small mammals and fruit.

LONGEST GESTATION PERIOD (MAMMAL)
Indian elephant (*Elephas maximus*)
20–22 months (average)

The Indian elephant gives birth to one calf which is suckled for at least four, and sometimes six, years.

SHORTEST GESTATION PERIOD (MAMMAL)
Virginia (Common) opossum (*Didelphis virginiana*)
13 days

Virginia opossums are marsupials and found in the USA and Canada. They have a grey/black coat, pointed snout and a long, prehensile tail.
Nocturnal and omnivorous, the Virginia opossum often feigns death when attacked, giving rise to the expression 'playing possum'.

LONGEST HIBERNATION
Hoary marmot (*Marmota caligata*)
Up to 9 months

Marmots are rodents (they have strong teeth for gnawing), are herbivorous and related to squirrels, but are heavier and more powerful. They are found in North America, Central Asia and Europe, where they live in close-knit family groups in a system of deep, interconnecting burrows. Generally round in shape, with brownish fur, marmots grow to a length of 11–23 in (30–60 cm), have stumpy, bushy tails and short legs.

LARGEST HORSE
Clydesdale/Shire
Up to 18 hands* high

The Clydesdale was used extensively in agricultural and timber work and also to haul coal from the local mines. Today it is used mainly on ceremonial occasions to pull brewers' drays, and as a drum horse in military parades. The Shire was used for hundreds of years as a basic 'carthorse'. Despite their size, Shires are gentle and willing.

SMALLEST HORSE
Falabella
Up to 7 hands* high

Falabellas were developed by the Falabella family in Argentina, and are partly derived from the Shetland pony. They are strong for their height and gentle in temperament. Falabellas are kept as pets and, although they are occasionally used as miniature carriage horses, they are not ridden.

*A hand is 4 in (10 cm)

LARGEST DOG
Height: Irish wolfhound 28–35 in (71–90 cm)
Weight: Mastiff 190–220 lb (86–100 kg)
The Irish wolfhound was probably introduced to Ireland by the Romans and the Irish chieftains soon took to them. They were used in hunting and for protection. The mastiff is slightly heavier than the St Bernard and was developed by the Romans as a fighting dog.

SMALLEST DOG
Chihuahua
6–9 in (15–23 cm) height, 2–6 lb (1–3 kg) weight
The Chihuahua takes its name from the Mexican state from where it was first exported to the USA. It is even-tempered and friendly, but its fragile frame means it needs careful handling.

LARGEST CAT
Maine Coon, Ragdoll
Up to 20 lb (9.1 kg)
The Maine coon is the oldest indigenous breed in the USA. Maine coons are powerfully built and muscular, and grow thick winter coats. The blue-eyed ragdoll is so-called because of its curious

The Chihuahua, weighing in at a maximum of 6 lb (3 kg), is the smallest dog in the world

habit of becoming completely relaxed when being stroked or picked up.

SMALLEST CAT
Singapura
6 lb (2.7 kg)

The Singapura was developed in the USA in the

1970s from the feral (half wild) cats of Singapore which live in the streets and are known locally as 'drain cats'. Singapuras are attractively coloured, cream or ivory, with bronze markings and have almond-shaped eyes. They are very rare and thus are extremely valuable.

TALLEST FLIGHTLESS BIRD
Ostrich (*Struthio camelus*)
Up to 8 ft (2.5 m) high (male)
The ostrich lives in the dry plains of East Africa and is omnivorous, eating mainly plants, fruits, seeds, leaves and shoots, although it will also take small animals, such as lizards. Ostriches, by virtue of their height, make good sentries and they often graze with herds of animals such as zebra and gnu, acting as early-warning lookouts. In return, the grazing animals disturb seeds and nuts for the ostriches.

TALLEST FLYING BIRD
Siberian crane (*Grus leucogeranus*)
Up to 5 ft (1.5 m) high
Cranes are found all over the world, on every continent except South America and Antarctica.

Cranes are most often found in open country, usually near water – marshes, lakes and the seashore. They eat fish, small animals, roots and fruits and can live to a great age. Although shy birds, they are very gregarious and migrate in large flocks. Several species are now threatened with extinction.

SMALLEST BIRD
Bee hummingbird (*Mellisuga helenae*)
2 in (5 cm)
The bee hummingbird of Cuba is smaller than some insects and weighs less than 0.07 oz (2 g).

HEAVIEST FLYING BIRD
Kori (giant) bustard (*Ardeotis kori*)
Up to 4 ft 6 in (1.34 m) long, up to 35 lb (16 kg) weight
The kori bustard resembles an ostrich or crane in appearance, and lives in dry, open country in east and south Africa, feeding on buds, leaves, seeds and insects. Its weight brings it near to the physical limits for flying and it flies only reluctantly and for short distances. On the other hand, it can run fast to escape predators.

LARGEST WINGSPAN
Wandering albatross (*Diomeda exulans*)
Over 11 ft 6 in (3.5 m)

The wandering albatross is a large, long-winged, gliding seabird, which feeds on most kinds of sea animal found near the surface of the water, and spends much of its time, when not breeding, in the air. Its characteristic gliding motion depends on air speeds and currents and its wings have the highest aspect ratio (proportion of length to breadth) of any bird, from 20 to 25.

The huge wingspan of the albatross enables it to glide over long distances, using varying air speeds and currents

FASTEST-FLYING BIRD (NON-DIVING SPEED)
Swifts

Swifts are the most aerial of birds, some even mating and passing the night on the wing. Their bodies are specially adapted for high-speed flying, with streamlined shape and short legs – although this means that the bird has great difficulty in launching itself off the ground if it should fall.

FASTEST-FLYING BIRD (DIVING SPEED)
Peregrine falcon (*Falco peregrinus*)
100–275 mph (160–440 km/h)

These figures are estimated speeds of a peregrine falcon's gravity-assisted dive or stoop (that is, the dive which the bird makes to catch its prey on the wing). Peregrine falcons are found on all continents except Antarctica and feed almost exclusively on other birds.

FASTEST WING BEAT
Hummingbirds (Family *Trochilidae*)
Up to 90 beats per second

Small hummingbirds, such as the vervain hummingbird, attain these speeds while hovering to gather nectar from a flower (*see* **SMALLEST BIRD**, *page 69*). It is said that even faster speeds (up to 200 beats a second) are attained during mating displays.

HIGHEST-FLYING BIRD
Ruppell's vulture (*Gyps rueppellii*)

No accurate measurements can be given for the height that these birds can attain, although individuals have been known to fly as high as an aeroplane. Vultures are gregarious, carrion-feeding birds living in open or mountainous terrain in hot countries in Africa, Asia and Europe. The birds soar to great heights, using air currents, then glide in immense circles looking for dead or dying animals on the ground, aided by their amazing eyesight – they can spot a carcass from several thousand feet up. Then they plummet like a stone to the ground and rush to the food with outstretched wings and neck.

FASTEST-SWIMMING BIRD
Emperor penguin (*Aptenodytes forsteri*)
10 knots (11 mph/20 km/h) (double these speeds for short bursts)

The flightless penguin is the most marine of birds; it can swim as fast as a seal and has webbed toes and wings that cannot be folded. Emperor penguins inhabit the Antarctic where they live on crustaceans, such as krill, fish and squid.

DEEPEST-DIVING BIRD
Emperor penguin (*Aptenodytes forsteri*)
880 ft (268 m)
This dive was measured by a depth recorder attached to the bird.

LARGEST BIRD'S NEST
Mallee fowl (*Leipoa ocellata*)
5 ft (1.5 m) high, 16 ft (5 m) diameter (above ground)
The male mallee fowl of southern Australia spends almost its entire life occupied with building and maintaining its nest, basically a hole about 3 ft (1 m) deep, filled with vegetation. After hatching, the chicks are left to fend for themselves, although they can fly within 24 hours of surfacing. Mallee fowl are quiet, shy birds and feed on seeds, buds and some insects.

SMALLEST BIRD'S NEST
Hummingbirds (Family *Trochilidae*)

The smallest hummingbirds, such as the tiny bee hummingbird (*see* **SMALLEST BIRD**, *page 69*), build minute, cup-shaped nests made from animal down, mosses and lichens held together with spider silk and saliva. They are attached to twigs, vines and the roofs of caves by plant fibres and usually contain two eggs.

The hummingbird is a triple record-holder, being the smallest bird and having the smallest nest and eggs. This Costas hummingbird was photographed in the Sonora Desert, Arizona, USA

LARGEST BIRD'S EGG
Ostrich (*Struthio camelus*)
6 in (15 cm) long, 5 in (13 cm) diameter, 3 lb (1.4 kg) weight

Ostriches lay their eggs in shallow pits in sandy soil about 3 ft (1 m) across. The pit is excavated by the male who also looks after the eggs and protects the chicks when they hatch. *See* **TALLEST FLIGHTLESS BIRD**, *page 68.*

SMALLEST BIRD'S EGG
Bee hummingbird (*Mellisuga helenae*)
0.3 in (7.5 mm) long

The eggs can weigh less than 0.02 oz (0.5 g) and take 12–19 days to hatch. *See* **SMALLEST BIRD, SMALLEST BIRD'S NEST**, *pages 69, 74.*

LARGEST FISH
Whale shark (*Rhincodon typus*)
Up to 50 ft (15 m) long

Despite its terrifying appearance, the whale shark is docile and harmless to man. It lives in warm seas such as the Atlantic, Pacific and Indian oceans, feeding on small planktonic animals which it ingests by filtering through a grille as it glides through the water.

SMALLEST FISH
Pygmy goby (*Pandaka pygmaea*)
Approx ¹/₂ in (1.2 cm)
The pygmy goby is a freshwater fish from the
Philippines and is the smallest known vertebrate
(animal with a backbone) in the world.

FISH LIVING AT GREATEST DEPTH
Brotulids
Up to 24,000 ft (7300 m) deep
There are some 200 species of brotulid, primitive
fish which live in the deepest seas. In general, they
have elongated, pointed tails, a single long,
spineless fin and range from a few inches or
centimetres to 3 ft (90 cm) in length. They inhabit
only deep waters and undersea caves, where there
is little if any light and, consequently, many
brotulids are sightless.

MOST POISONOUS FISH
**Weever fish (*Trachinus draco*), stonefish
(*Synaceia horrida*)**
Found in the Mediterranean Sea, the deadly
weever fish carries a toxic cocktail in its opercula
(bony flaps covering the gill slits) and dorsal fin

which, if touched, can kill human beings. The chemistry of the poison is not yet known and there is no antidote. The stonefish is found in shallow, tropical waters in the Indian and Pacific oceans. Its dorsal spines have bulbous, poison-filled glands at their bases, which the fish can eject when threatened. This powerful neurotoxin (nerve poison) can be fatal to humans, and is known to have killed bathers who have accidentally trodden on stonefish in the shallow waters off northern Australia.

LARGEST JELLYFISH
Arctic giant (*Cyanea arctica*)
Up to 90 in (2.28 m) bell diameter, 120 ft (36.5 m) tentacles
The Arctic giant is the longest animal in the world. It lives in the north-east Atlantic and swims by rhythmically pulsating the bell. The tentacles and bell are covered with stinging cells which paralyse the prey trapped by the tentacles.

MOST POISONOUS JELLYFISH
Seawasps (*Chironex* and *Chiropsalmus*)
Seawasps live in the Indian Ocean between

Australia and Malaysia, and are also found in shallow waters off the Pacific coast of Queensland, Australia. Their venom can kill a human within three minutes.

MOST POISONOUS MOLLUSC
Spotted octopus (*Octopus maculosus*)

The spotted octopus lives in the Indo-Pacific and Indian oceans and produces a powerful cephalotoxin, a neuromuscular poison, which causes stinging pain, numbness in the mouth and neck, blurring of the vision, paralysis, coma and, usually, death.

LARGEST TOAD
Cane toad (*Bufo marinus*)
Up to 9 in (23 cm) long, 1 lb (450 g) weight

The cane toad is also called the marine, giant and Mexican toad. The genus *Bufo* is found all over the world, except in Antarctica, Madagascar and Polynesia. If threatened, the cane toad produces noxious secretions on its skin and can squirt poison from glands behind its eyes up to 3 ft (1 m) away. These poisons have been known to kill dogs, and even in human adults can cause temporary paralysis.

LARGEST TOAD IN UK
Common toad (*Bufo bufo*)
Up to 6 in (15 cm)

The common toad has a compact body and short legs; it can both walk and hop. Its skin is thick, dry and warty – not slimy – and it has poison glands behind its eyes and in the warts on its back, although these pose no threat to humans. There are only two species of toad in the UK; the other is the natterjack (*Bufo calamita*).

LARGEST FROG
Goliath frog (*Conraua goliath*)
Up to 1 ft (30 cm) long, 7¼ lb (3.3 kg) weight

The Goliath frog is also known as the West African giant frog or *Gigantorana goliath*.

SMALLEST FROG
Brazilian *brachycephalids*
½ in (10 mm) long

MOST POISONOUS FROG
Koikoi (poison-arrow frog) (*Phyllobates bicolor*)

The poison-arrow frog is a native of the rainforests of Colombia, South America. Its poison is deadly;

it is estimated that 0.0000004 oz (0.00001 g) can kill a human.

LONGEST SNAKE
Reticulated python (*Python reticulata*)
Up to 33 ft (10 m) long

The reticulated python lives in the humid rainforests and bushy scrublands of south-east Asia. It is heavy as well as long and weighs some 220 lb (100 kg). The python feeds on birds and mammals and can kill animals as large as pigs and small deer. The reticulated python does not bite, but coils itself around the prey and squeezes it with its immensely powerful muscles until the animal is suffocated.

FASTEST SNAKE
Black mamba (*Dendroaspis polylepis*)
Up to 7 mph (11 km/h), short bursts over level ground

A native of central and southern Africa, the tree-dwelling black mamba grows to about 14 ft (4.5 m) long and is very poisonous; the venom can kill a human within ten minutes. Black mambas attack with great ferocity and rush with unbelievable speed on their victims, which have little chance of escape.

MOST POISONOUS SNAKE (MARINE)
Sea snake (*Hydrophis belcheri*)
Most sea snakes live off the coasts of Asia and northern Australia. Their venom is far more powerful than that of any land snake.

MOST POISONOUS SNAKE (TERRESTRIAL)
Taipan (*Oxyuranus scutellatus*)
The taipan grows to some 11 ft (3.3 m) and inhabits Australia and New Guinea. Its bite causes blood-clotting leading to general paralysis and is fatal within minutes.

LARGEST REPTILE
Komodo dragon (*Varanus komodoensis*)
Up to 10 ft (3 m) long, 135 lb (61 kg) weight
The komodo dragon is a type of monitor lizard and inhabits a few small islands in Indonesia. Despite its size, the komodo can run very fast and is a dangerous predator, readily attacking large animals such as pigs, deer and buffaloes. Its method is

simple: it bites through the tendons on the animal's legs and brings it to the ground. The komodo dragon has a voracious appetite and will devour its own kind as well as eating carrion, when available. It is now an endangered species.

LARGEST SPIDER
Goliath bird-eating spider (*Theraphosa leblondi*)
Up to 10 in (25 cm) diameter

The Goliath spider lives in the South American rainforests, particularly around the Amazon basin, and the Guianas. It consumes birds, insects, frogs, toads, mice and lizards. In captivity, the spiders can grow even larger; claims have been made for a 11 in (25.5 cm) legspan and a weight of 6 oz (170 g).

SMALLEST SPIDER
Patu marplesi
0.1 in (2.5 mm)

This microscopic spider is a native of Western Samoa.

LARGEST SPIDER'S WEB
Orb-weaving spiders
Up to 5 ft (1.5 m) diameter, up to 20 ft (6 m) supporting threads

The tropical orb-weavers produce the largest webs, made from very strong silk which is a beautiful golden colour. Attempts were made to breed the spiders and use the silk for manufacturing fabric, but they proved difficult to rear and tended to eat each other.

MOST POISONOUS SPIDER
Brazilian huntsman (*Phoneutria fera*)
The Brazilian huntsman is a member of the Ctenidae family, a small group of mainly tropical and subtropical spiders, known as wandering spiders. Normally they pose no real threat to humans, but they sometimes hide in clothes and shoes and can inflict several painful, poisonous bites when disturbed. If treated promptly with the anti-venom, the bite will not prove fatal.

LARGEST SCORPION
Emperor (imperial) scorpion (*Pandinus imperator*)
Up to 8 in (20 cm) long
Scorpions are classed, like spiders, as arachnids, and inhabit mainly hot, dry regions such as north Africa, the Middle East, Asia, Australia and the Americas.

SMALLEST SCORPION
Microbothus pusillus
1/2 in (13 mm) long
Scorpions have elongated bodies and a segmented tail ending in a sharp stinger. They have four pairs of legs, variously used for walking and for grasping and tearing apart their prey. Large prey is usually paralysed by the venom in the stinger before the scorpion rips it open and sucks out the juices.

MOST POISONOUS SCORPION
Fat-tailed scorpion (*Androctonus australis*)
The fat-tailed scorpion of Tunisia produces a neurotoxin (nerve poison) which causes paralysis of the heart and respiratory muscles and can prove fatal to children and old people.

LONGEST INSECT
Stick insects (*Palophus, Pharnacia*)
Up to 1 ft 1 in (33 cm) long
Leaf-eating stick insects are superbly adapted to their environment; their body shape and colour reflects that of the twigs and branches they live among, and they carry warts and spines on their skin resembling buds and prickles. Most stick

insects (also called walkingsticks) are nocturnal
feeders and remain absolutely motionless during
the day.

SMALLEST INSECT
Feather-winged beetles (*Nanosella fungi*)
0.01 in (0.25 mm) long
These minute insects are known as feather-winged
beetles because the membrane on the wings has been
replaced with a dense layer of fringed hairs. Feather-
wings live in tropical regions and inhabit rotting
wood, fungi, manure, ant nests or the bark of trees.

HEAVIEST INSECT
African goliath beetle (*Goliathus giganteus*)
Up to 4 in (10 cm) long, up to $3^1/_2$ oz (99 g)
weight
The goliath beetle has black, leathery wings, bigger
than those of a small bird. It lives in equatorial
Africa.

INSECT WITH SHORTEST LIFESPAN
Mayfly (*Cloeon dipterum*)
Lifespan of a few hours as mature adult
Mayflies live underwater as grubs or nymphs,

feeding on water plants. After two to three years, the nymph comes to the surface of the water, its skin splits and it emerges in its adult form as a mayfly. The insect sheds its skin once more and then flies away. The mayfly lives long enough only to mate and lay eggs.

PRECIOUS STONES AND GOLD

LARGEST DIAMOND
Cullinan Diamond
3106 carats* or 1¹/₄ lb (621 g)

The Cullinan Diamond was mined on 26 January 1905 in Pretoria, South Africa. It was cut into nine principal stones, of which Cullinan I, the 'Great Star of Africa' (74 facets), was set into the British royal sceptre, and Cullinan II (64 facets) into the Imperial State Crown. Both of these can be seen in the Tower of London. Diamonds are the hardest of all gems (10 on Mohs' hardness scale) and were formed from carbon millions of years ago.

LARGEST RUBY
Approx 250 carats* or 1 ³/₄ oz (50 g)

The largest known gem-quality ruby is found in the St Wenceslas crown which Charles IV of Luxembourg, King of Bavaria, placed on the skull

---

* In precious stones, a carat defines weight: one
  carat = 0.2 g or 200 mg

The Cullinan Diamond is the largest diamond in the world, although it was cut into nine principal stones soon after it had been mined in 1905

of the saint in his shrine. Rubies are a gem-variety of corundum and vary from deep to pale rose-red. The most valuable colour is known as 'pigeon-blood' and has a touch of blue.

LARGEST EMERALD (CRYSTAL)
16,300 carats* or 7.13 lb (3260 g)

This crystal, together with one of 6550 carats or 2.87 lb/1310 g, is mounted in the handle of a dagger in the Topkapi Museum in Istanbul, Turkey, famous for its collection of emeralds. Emeralds are a deep green variety of beryl.

LARGEST SAPPHIRE (CRYSTAL)
63,000 carats* or 27.6 lb (12,600 g)

This magnificent crystal was discovered in Myanmar (formerly Burma) in 1966. Sapphires are a gem-variety of corundum and the most prized sapphires are blue, although colours can range from white and yellow to violet, green and black.

---

* In precious stones, a carat defines weight: one carat = 0.2 g or 200 mg

LARGEST OPAL
Panther Opal
281,500 carats* or 123.1 lb (56.3 kg)

The Panther Opal was mined in Australia at the beginning of the century, during the 'opal rush' in Queensland and New South Wales. Opals are composed of hydrated silica and are unique among gems, being neither completely opaque nor completely transparent. Colours vary from greenish red (fire opal), black or white (cacholong) to a combination of several colours (harlequin).

LARGEST PEARL
Hope Pearl
450 carats* or 3.15 oz (90 g)

The Hope Pearl is about 2 in (5 cm) long and is named after the banker Henry Philip Hope. Even larger pearls, such as the Pearl of Asia (575 carats or 4.03 oz/115 g) and the Pearl of Allah (32,000 carats or 14 lb/6.4 kg) are cited in some sources. Pearls are formed within the shells of certain

---

*In precious stones, a carat defines weight: one carat = 0.2 g or 200 mg

molluscs (such as oysters and mussels) when layers of calcium carbonate form round a foreign body which irritates the animal. Colours can vary from silvery-white and cream to rose, grey and black.

LARGEST MASS OF GOLD
Holtermann Nugget
4 ft 9 in (1.45 m) high; 1 ft 3 in (38 cm) wide; 557 $^3/_4$ lb (235 kg) weight

The Holtermann Nugget, a huge lump of mixed slate and gold, was found in the Beyers and Holtermann Star of Hope mine at Hill End, New South Wales, Australia on 19 October 1872. It yielded over 197 lb (90 kg) of pure gold.

LARGEST NUGGET
Welcome Stranger
150.9 lb (69 kg)

The largest gold nugget ever found came to light quite by accident, exposed in the ruts of a cart track near Dunolly, Victoria, Australia in 1869. Gold is a heavy, soft metal (between 2$^1/_2$ and 3 on Mohs' hardness scale) and is one of only two metals that, in its pure form, is neither grey nor white (copper is the other). The purity of gold is expressed in carats on a scale of 24, where 24 is pure gold.

COUNTRIES OF THE WORLD

LARGEST COUNTRY
Russia
6,592,800 miles^2 (17,075,352 km^2)

The population of Russia is approximately 149,000,000 and includes 75 different races. As a result of the 1917 Russian Revolution, Russia became part of the Union of Soviet Socialist Republics (USSR) from 1922 to the dissolution of the USSR in 1991. The capital is Moscow.

SMALLEST COUNTRY
Vatican City State
0.2 miles^2 (0.51 km^2)

Vatican City State is an independent country within the city of Rome. It is the residence of the pope, head of the Roman Catholic Church. The pope has absolute power over the administration of this tiny country and appoints all the government officers. The population is about 1000.

COUNTRY WITH HIGHEST POPULATION
China (excluding Taiwan)
1,208,842,000

The People's Republic of China has an area of
approximately 3,705,408 miles^2 (9,597,006 km^2).
The Chinese government has introduced policies to
try and curb the population growth, penalizing
couples who have more than one child.

COUNTRY WITH LOWEST POPULATION
Vatican City State
Approx 1000

See SMALLEST COUNTRY, *page 93.*

MOST DENSELY POPULATED COUNTRY
Monaco
31,000 people per 0.4 miles^2 (20,800 people per km^2)

Monaco-Ville is the capital of this small principality
on the Mediterranean coast, whose land adjoins
French territory on every side.

MOST SPARSELY POPULATED COUNTRY
Greenland
1 person per 15.1 miles^2 (1 person per 39.1 km^2)

The population of Greenland is just under 56,000 and the area is 840,000 miles^2 (2,175,600 km^2). It is an internally self-governing part of Denmark. The capital is Nuuk (Godthåb) and the population is made up of indigenous Eskimos (Inuit) and Danish settlers.

HIGHEST LIFE-EXPECTANCY (FEMALE)
85.3 years
Republic of San Marino

The population of San Marino, the third smallest independent country in Europe after Vatican City State and Monaco, is about 25,000 and the area about 23 miles^2 (61 km^2). It is on the Italian peninsula. The UK life-expectancy for females is 80 years.

HIGHEST LIFE-EXPECTANCY (MALE)
77.1 years
Iceland

Iceland is a large island in the northern Atlantic Ocean. Over half the population lives in and around the capital, Reykjavik. Iceland is a very prosperous country with a high standard of living and excellent health and education services. The UK life-expectancy for males is 75 years.

LOWEST LIFE-EXPECTANCY (MALE AND FEMALE)
36.4 years female, 35.9 years male
Rwanda

Rwanda is a small republic in central Africa. When the country became independent in 1962 (it was formerly administered by Belgium), civil war flared up between the Tutsi (Watutsi) and Hutu people and continued to do so from time to time, damaging the country's already fragile economy. In 1994, the Rwandan president was assassinated and the civil war was resumed. The situation continues to be unstable and there seems little prospect, at the moment, of improving the health and welfare conditions of the Rwandan people. For comparison, the UK life-expectancy for males is 75 years and for females 80 years.

COUNTRY WITH YOUNGEST POPULATION (PERCENTAGE OF POPULATION UNDER 15)
Marshall Islands
51 per cent

The Marshall Islands form an independent

republic in the central Pacific. The indigenous
people are Micronesians and the population is
around 58,000. The Marshall Islanders have large
families (the average number of births for a woman
of childbearing age is seven) and the doubling time
for the population is only 18 years.

COUNTRY WITH OLDEST POPULATION (PERCENTAGE OF PEOPLE OVER 75)
Monaco
10.8 per cent
See MOST DENSELY POPULATED COUNTRY, *page 94.*

RICHEST COUNTRY
Luxembourg
£24,900 GNP per head (US $39,850)
The GNP (Gross National Product) is a very rough
measure of the annual average national income per
person. Luxembourg is a small, landlocked country
of some 999 miles² (2587 km²), lying between
Belgium, France and Germany. The only large
town is also called Luxembourg. Luxembourg is an
independent Grand Duchy with a population of
around 381,000.

POOREST COUNTRY
Rwanda and Mozambique
£50 GNP per head (US $80)

The GNP (Gross National Product) is a very rough measure of the annual average national income per person. For Rwanda, *see* **LOWEST LIFE-EXPECTANCY (MALE AND FEMALE)**, *page 96*. Mozambique, on the coast of south-east Africa, is a former Portuguese colony which became independent in 1975. Unfortunately, years of civil war since independence have taken their toll on the economy, which was further shaken by a severe drought and subsequent famine in 1992.

LARGEST CITY
Mexico City, Mexico
Population 15,000,000

Mexico City is built on the site of the ancient Aztec capital, Tenochtitlan. It lies at an altitude of 7350 ft (2240 m).

LARGEST CITY IN EUROPE
Paris, France
Population 9,300,000

Paris, on the River Seine, has a history which goes

back over 2000 years. The city's population is made up of some two million residents of the centre, Ville de Paris, and the seven million residents of the 20 districts (*arrondissements*).

LARGEST CITY IN THE UK
London, England
Population 7,000,000
London (Londinium) on the River Thames was founded by the Romans in about AD 43. London is composed of the City of London (now mainly offices) and 32 boroughs, which make up Greater London.

LARGEST CITY IN NORTH AMERICA
Mexico City, Mexico
Population 15,000,000
See **LARGEST CITY**, *page 98.*

LARGEST CITY IN SOUTH AMERICA
Buenos Aires, Argentina
Population 10,000,000
Buenos Aires ('Fair Winds') was first settled by Europeans in 1580 and lies 124 miles (199.6 km) from the sea on the Rio de la Plata (River Plate).

LARGEST CITY IN AFRICA
Cairo, Egypt
Population 13,000,000

Cairo, on the River Nile, was the centre of the
Ancient Egyptian civilization, and modern Cairo
dates back to the 10th century. The city has grown
rapidly in recent years and remains the most
important centre for trade between Europe, the
Middle East and North Africa.

LARGEST CITY IN ASIA
Bombay, India
Population 12,500,000

Bombay (now called Mumbai) is the financial,
trading and film industry centre of India. Known
as the 'Gateway to India', it is one of the most
densely-populated cities in the world.

LARGEST CITY IN AUSTRALASIA
Sydney, Australia
Population 3,770,000

The city was founded in 1788 by a group of
convicts and soldiers who came ashore nearby. It
was the first European settlement in Australia and
was named after Viscount Sydney, the British

government minister responsible for colonial
affairs at the time.

HUMAN LIFE AND SOCIETY

TALLEST KNOWN PERSON
Robert Pershing Wadlow
8 ft 11 in (2.71 m)

Wadlow was born in Illinois, USA, and died in 1940 at the age of 22. Gigantism is a rare abnormality of growth which causes the sufferer to grow to an excessive height. The underlying medical cause is an abnormality of the pituitary gland which secretes an excess of growth hormone. People with gigantism are not physically strong and may have a shortened life-expectancy.

SHORTEST KNOWN PERSON
Gul Mohammed
22 1/2 in (56.3 cm)

Mohammed was born in India in 1957 and died in 1997. Like gigantism, dwarfism or restricted growth can be caused by hormonal disturbances or problems with the pituitary gland, but it can also be inherited.

Being measured for a suit turned into a major undertaking for Robert Wadlow, the world's tallest person, who unfortunately died at the early age of 22 in 1940

LONGEST BONE IN THE BODY
Femur
The femur is a legbone which joins the hip joint to
the knee joint. The 206 bones of the human body
support and protect the vital organs. A healthy
human bone is almost as strong as cast iron or
steel, but only a fraction of their weight. Bones can
repair and regenerate themselves when damaged.

LARGEST ORGAN IN THE HUMAN BODY
Skin
$21^1/_2$ ft^2 (2 m^2) per average adult
All vertebrates (animals with backbones) have skin,
although the outer covering is different in different
species (scales, hair, feathers, etc.). The skin is a
multifunctional organ, protecting body tissues against
injury, regulating body temperature and providing a
waterproof outer layer. Receptor nerves in the skin
are constantly sending messages to the brain.

LARGEST CONSTITUENT OF THE HUMAN BODY
Water
60.8 pints (38 litres) per average adult
Water is the main component of blood and the

average adult has between 6.2 and 10.6 pints (3.5–6 litres) of blood. Each day the body loses about 0.44 pints (0.25 litres) in sweat.

OLDEST KNOWN PERSON
Jeanne Louise Calment, 122 years (died 1997)

MOST CHILDREN IN A SINGLE BIRTH (SURVIVING)
Seven (4 boys, 3 girls)

The McCaughey septuplets were born on 19 November 1997 in Des Moines, Iowa, USA. The babies were carried for longer than 31 weeks (the longest-known period for such a large multiple pregnancy), and all seven babies weighed more than the critical weight of 2 lb (0.9 kg).

OLDEST KNOWN MOTHER
Rosanna Dalla Corta, Italy, 63

A son, born in July 1994. The mother is said to have undergone fertility treatment.

OLDEST KNOWN MOTHER IN THE UK
Elizabeth Buttle, England, 60

A son, born in January 1998. The mother is said to have undergone fertility treatment.

MOST COMMON CAUSE OF DEATH (DEVELOPED COUNTRIES)
Diseases of the circulatory system (heart disease and stroke)

These so-called 'diseases of civilization', such as coronary heart disease, are associated with over-eating, lack of exercise and smoking. The commonest type of heart disease causes narrowing and stiffening of the coronary arteries (those that supply the heart muscle with blood). If an artery is completely blocked by a blood clot, then the heart muscle is damaged and the heart itself may fail. A reduction of blood flow to a part of the brain, resulting from the lodging of a blood clot in an artery in the brain, is described as a stroke; temporary or permanent paralysis of parts of the body may result.

COUNTRY WITH HIGHEST DEATH RATE FROM CIRCULATORY DISEASES
Hungary
676 per 100,000 population

The comparable rate in the UK is 507 per 100,000 population.

COUNTRY WITH LOWEST DEATH RATE FROM CIRCULATORY DISEASES
Japan
144 per 100,000 population
The comparable rate in the UK is 507 per 100,000 population.

RAREST DISEASE
Smallpox (variola)
Smallpox was officially declared eradicated in 1980 after a world vaccination programme launched by the World Health Organization. Smallpox causes fever, muscle pains and a severe rash of weeping pustules which leave deep, pitted scars; it is often, but not always, fatal. Some smallpox cultures are still kept in laboratories for research purposes.

MOST COMMON DISEASE
Common cold
There are almost 200 different rhinoviruses which cause the common cold and, as they have a tendency to mutate, their numbers are constantly increasing.

MOST RECENTLY-DISCOVERED DISEASE
New strain of Creutzfeldt-Jacob Disease (CJD)

Creutzfeldt-Jacob Disease causes dementia (mental deterioration), is irreversible and always fatal. It may possibly be transmitted to humans by eating meat infected with BSE (bovine spongiform encephalitis), a similar disease which affects cattle.

MOST RAPIDLY-INCREASING DISEASE
Tuberculosis

Tuberculosis kills more people every year than AIDS and malaria combined. Once the scourge of western industrialized societies, particularly in the 19th century, the disease is spreading rapidly in developing countries and has also begun to reappear in the West, especially in impoverished inner-city areas. Humans are usually infected by the *Mycobacterium tuberculosis* bacillus, which is air-borne and expelled from the lungs of infected people. The bacilli affect the lungs, causing lumps or tubercles to form; the lungs become scarred, the patient's health deteriorates and there is a persistent cough. Whole areas of the lungs are slowly destroyed, the patient suffers considerable pain and coughs up blood, becoming progressively weaker until eventually dying from general debility.

LONGEST-REIGNING MONARCH IN EUROPEAN HISTORY
Louis XIV of France 1643–1715
72 years

Louis XIV came to power at the age of four years and eight months. His early years were dominated

Louis XIV of France enjoyed a record-breaking reign of 72 years. This painting by Louis de Silvestre shows the monarch greeting the Elector of Saxony to Fontainebleau in 1714, the year before his death

by Cardinal Mazarin, who wielded absolute control over Louis. When Mazarin died in 1661 the king, aged 23, assumed complete and unchallenged authority over his kingdom. A great patron of the arts, Louis built the vast court at Versailles and encouraged writers such as Racine and Molière. Although he was accused of ruining the country through his extravagance and his constant wars with neighbouring countries, in an attempt to consolidate French supremacy, Louis, the Sun King, left an invaluable artistic legacy to the French people.

LONGEST-REIGNING MONARCH IN THE UK
Victoria 1837–1901
64 years

Victoria became queen at the age of 18 and, three years later, married the German Prince Albert. The couple were very happy together, producing nine children, and Victoria was devastated by Albert's death in 1861 at the age of 42. The Golden Jubilee, celebrating 50 years of her rule in 1887, marked the zenith of British power and wealth. Victoria's presence so marked the 19th century that her name has become synonymous with it.

Victoria is the longest-reigning monarch of the United Kingdom. This portrait appeared in The Times *to celebrate her Diamond Jubilee in 1897*

FIRST BRITISH PRIME MINISTER
Robert Walpole

Sir Robert Walpole is widely accepted as having established the office and role of prime minister, although this title did not exist at the time. Although Walpole recognized the growing influence of the House of Commons in formulating government policies, he made extensive personal use of government patronage (offering titles, jobs or gifts to gain someone's support) to ensure he got sufficient backing for his plans. He will always be remembered for saying 'All men have their price.'

YOUNGEST BRITISH PRIME MINISTER
William Pitt the Younger
Prime Minister in 1783, aged 24

William Pitt was one of the country's greatest statesmen – but he is also credited as the man who introduced the first income tax (at 10 per cent), to help to pay for the wars against Napoleon. *See* **YOUNGEST MALE MEMBER OF PARLIAMENT, YOUNGEST GRADUATE IN THE UK,** *pages 115, 117.*

LONGEST-SERVING BRITISH PRIME MINISTER
Robert Banks Jenkinson, 2nd Earl of Liverpool
Prime Minister 1812–27

The Earl of Liverpool came to power after the death of Spencer Perceval (*see below*, **FIRST BRITISH PRIME MINISTER TO BE ASSASSINATED**). Liverpool steered the country through the war with America in 1812 and the final campaigns of the Napoleonic wars.

FIRST BRITISH PRIME MINISTER TO BE ASSASSINATED
Spencer Perceval, murdered on 11 May 1812

Spencer Perceval was shot in the House of Commons entrance by a bankrupt businessman from Liverpool, John Bellingham, who blamed government policies for his failures. He was later hanged for his crime.

FIRST FEMALE PRIME MINISTER
Sirimavo Bandaranaike
Prime Minister of Sri Lanka (1960–64, 1970–77, 1994–)

Sirimavo Bandaranaike was married to the

politician Solomon Bandaranaike in 1940, and
when he was assassinated in 1959 she became party
leader. Her Sri Lanka Freedom Party won a
decisive victory in the General Election of July
1960 and she became the world's first female prime
minister.

FIRST FEMALE PRIME MINISTER IN EUROPE
Margaret Thatcher
Prime Minister of Great Britain (1979–90)
Margaret Thatcher became party leader then prime
minister when her party won the general elections
of 1979, 1983 and 1987. Thatcher held strong
views on political principles and policies and
exerted considerable control over her ministers.
She was known as the 'Iron Lady'.

FIRST FEMALE MEMBER OF PARLIAMENT TO TAKE HER SEAT (HOUSE OF COMMONS)*
Viscountess (Nancy) Astor
Member of Parliament for Plymouth, 1919
Nancy Astor was elected as Unionist member for
Plymouth in 1919. As an MP, Astor took a great
interest in matters involving children, the family
and women's welfare and was highly regarded in

many spheres of society. The mother of six children, Nancy Astor was re-elected many times before she finally retired in 1945.

*Constance Gore-Booth (Countess Markievicz) was elected in 1918 to represent St Patrick's Division, Dublin, thus making her the first woman to be elected to the British parliament. In accordance with Sinn Fein policy, she did not take up her seat.

YOUNGEST MALE MEMBER OF PARLIAMENT
William Pitt the Younger
Member of Parliament in 1781, aged 22
William Pitt was the second son of the Earl of Chatham. He was educated privately, because of his poor health, until he entered the University of Cambridge at the age of 14. At 17 he graduated and in 1781 became MP for Appleby. *See* YOUNGEST BRITISH PRIME MINISTER, YOUNGEST GRADUATE IN THE UK, *pages 112, 117.*

YOUNGEST FEMALE MEMBER OF PARLIAMENT
(Josephine) Bernadette Devlin (McAliskey)

Member of Parliament in 1969, aged 22 years 359 days

As Bernadette Devlin, McAliskey (born 1947) became the MP for Mid-Ulster from 1969 to 1974, and was the youngest member since William Pitt the Younger (*see above*).

FIRST COUNTRY TO GIVE WOMEN THE RIGHT TO VOTE
New Zealand 1893

FIRST EUROPEAN COUNTRY TO GIVE WOMEN THE RIGHT TO VOTE
Finland 1906

LAST EUROPEAN COUNTRY TO GIVE WOMEN THE RIGHT TO VOTE
Liechtenstein 1984

YOUNGEST UNDERGRADUATE IN THE UK
William Thomson
Entered Glasgow University in 1834, aged 10

William Thomson had an outstanding career, combining pure and applied science and making important contributions to electromagnetism and thermodynamics. Thomson was knighted and

Painted in 1782, the year after he became the youngest male MP, William Pitt the Younger also holds the records for youngest graduate and youngest prime minister

became the first Baron Kelvin. He is buried in Westminster Abbey.

YOUNGEST GRADUATE IN THE UK

William Pitt the Younger
Graduated from Cambridge University in 1776, aged 17

See YOUNGEST BRITISH PRIME MINISTER, YOUNGEST MALE MEMBER OF PARLIAMENT, *pages 112, 115.*

YOUNGEST PROFESSOR IN THE UK
Colin Maclaurin
Professor of Mathematics, Marischal College, Aberdeen University, September 1717, aged 19
Scotsman Maclaurin graduated from Glasgow University in 1713.

RICHEST PERSON
Bill Gates
Estimated fortune £56 billion (1999)
American Gates is the founder of the computer software giant, Microsoft. Microsoft is currently valued at over £140 billion and has an annual revenue of over £11 billion.

SCIENCE & TECHNOLOGY

MOST COMMON ELEMENT* IN THE UNIVERSE

Hydrogen

Atomic number 1 Chemical symbol H

Hydrogen is the most common element in the universe and the third most common element after oxygen (46.6 per cent) and silicon (27.7 per cent) in the earth's crust. Hydrogen has no taste or smell and is invisible.

SIMPLEST NATURALLY-OCCURRING ELEMENT*

Hydrogen

Atomic number 1 Chemical symbol H

Hydrogen, a colourless gas, has only $1/15$ th of the weight of air and is so light that it was often used for fuelling balloons and airships – it has now been replaced by helium (the second-lightest element) which is not explosive, unlike hydrogen.

---

* An element is a substance which cannot be split into two or more substances by chemical experiment.

MOST COMPLEX NATURALLY-OCCURRING ELEMENT*
Uranium
Atomic number 92 Chemical symbol U
Uranium is a radioactive, silvery-white, metallic element. It is used chiefly as a source of nuclear energy by fission of the radioisotope uranium-235.

NEWEST ELEMENTS*
Transuranic elements
Atomic numbers 93–112
The transuranic elements are those which lie beyond uranium, number 92 in the periodic table of the elements. These elements, with the exception of plutonium, neptunium and americium, minute amounts of which have been found in nature, are artificial, radioactive, highly unstable and have lifespans ranging from billions of years to infinitesimal fractions of a second.

---

*An element is a substance which cannot be split into two or more substances by chemical experiment.

ELEMENT* WITH HIGHEST BOILING AND MELTING POINTS
Tungsten
Boiling point 10,652 °F (5900 °C)
Melting point 6098 °F (3370 °C)
Atomic number 74 Chemical symbol W
Tungsten or wolfram is a grey, solid metal. It is both malleable and hard and, alloyed with steel, is used for making the tips of high-speed cutting tools. The pure metal is used as a filament in electric light bulbs.

ELEMENT* WITH LOWEST BOILING AND MELTING POINTS
Helium
Boiling point −452.16 °F (−268.98 °C) Melting point −520.52 °F (−271.4 °C) at 29.6 atmospheres pressure
Helium is a colourless gas. In its liquid form it is the only liquid which cannot be frozen by reducing

*An element is a substance which cannot be split into two or more substances by chemical experiment.

temperature alone – pressure must also be applied. It is the second most abundant element in the universe.

LIGHTEST METAL
Lithium
Atomic number 3 Chemical symbol Li
Lithium is a silvery solid, used to harden alloys and in batteries. Lithium compounds are used in medicine to help sufferers from manic depression.

DENSEST METAL
Osmium
Atomic number 76 Chemical symbol Os
Osmium, a hard, bluish-white metal, is used to create a very hard alloy, used in instrument pivots and pen tips. Osmium is highly toxic.

LARGEST SUPERCOMPUTER
US Department of Energy Ultra computer, Sandia National Laboratories, New Mexico, USA
Introduced in 1996, this computer has the capacity to carry out 1 trillion calculations per second (teraflops). It is used to develop simulation technologies to ensure the safety and reliability of

the US nuclear deterrence without underground
testing, as well as providing the power for medical
and pharmaceutical research, weather prediction
and aircraft and car design.

LARGEST SUPERCOMPUTER IN THE UK
T3E Cray Supercomputer, Bracknell, England

The Cray Supercomputer is owned and operated
by the Meteorological Office. At the time of
writing, the Cray is the third biggest
supercomputer in the world and is used for
weather forecasting. Weather observations from all
over the world are fed into the computer which
converts them into mathematical equations and
then into forecasts. The Cray can make 80,000
million calculations per second.

LARGEST COMPUTER NETWORK
Internet

A computer network is a group of computers that
can be linked to each other to exchange
information. The 1990s saw the rapid growth of
commercial Internet-access providers and the
World Wide Web, offering users access to

information and contacts across the world. There are now hundreds of millions of Internet users, and the numbers are increasing daily.

ENERGY

LARGEST OILFIELD
Al-Ghawar, Saudi Arabia
82 billion barrels* (estimated)

Saudi Arabia has the largest oil reserves in the world (estimated 260 billion barrels). Oil is a fossil fuel, an organic material derived from long-dead organisms. Fossil fuels, such as oil, bitumen, natural gas and coal, are non-renewable sources of energy, yet provide over 80 per cent of our current energy needs. It is now thought that only some 23 per cent of recoverable deposits of oil remain.

LONGEST OIL PIPELINE
Trans-Alaskan pipeline
800 miles (1287 km)

The Trans-Alaskan pipeline runs from Prudhoe Bay on the north coast of Alaska to the ice-free port of Valdez, from where the oil is taken by tankers to ports on the west coast of the United States. The pipeline crosses three mountain ranges, 250 watercourses and,

---

* One barrel of oil = 35 gallons (159 litres)

for almost half the way, is suspended above the frozen
ground. Elsewhere, the pipeline is laid under the
permanently frozen ground, and insulated to prevent
any thawing of permafrost which would greatly alter
the environment.

LARGEST NATURAL GAS DEPOSITS
Urengoy, Siberia, Russia
285,000,000,000,000 ft^3 (8,087,000,000,000 m^3)

Urengoy lies on the Gulf of Ob in west Siberia on
the Arctic Circle. There are 15 separate reservoirs of
gas in the field and production began in 1978. Like
oil, natural gas is a non-renewable fossil fuel, derived
from plants and water-borne organic material.

LONGEST NATURAL GAS PIPELINE
Trans-Siberian pipeline
3750 miles (6034 km)

The Trans-Siberian pipeline links the huge Siberian
gas fields with western Europe, crossing over more
than 700 rivers and streams on its way.

LARGEST DAM (BY HEIGHT)
Rogun, Tajikistan
1099 ft (355 m)

LARGEST DAM (BY SIZE OF RESERVOIR)
Owen Falls, Uganda
9,540,000,000 ft³ (2,700,000,000 m³)

LARGEST DAM (BY POWER CAPACITY)
Turukhansk, Russia
20,000 megawatts

LARGEST RESERVOIR
Bratsk (Bratskoye), Russia
410 ft (125 m) high; 14,488 ft (4416 m) at widest;
137,230,000 acre ft (169,300,000,000 m³)
reservoir capacity

Bratsk is a large, hydro-electric power station with a power capacity of 4,500 megawatts. It was completed in 1964 and its very existence is a tribute to both the designers and the men who constructed it. The conditions in this remote and isolated area meant that men were working in temperatures as low as −72 °F (−58 °C) for considerable periods of time, with frost on over 280 days of the year.

LARGEST WATER PIPELINE
13 ft (4 m) diameter

Great Man-Made River Project, Libya, Africa

The Great Man-Made River Project (GMR) is designed to bring high-quality water, for both human and agricultural purposes, from sources deep under the Sahara desert to settlements along the Libyan coast. It was begun in 1983, but will not be complete until 2007.

FIRST MAJOR TIDAL POWER STATION
Rance, France (1966)

The Rance power station measures 0.5 miles (804 m) across and has 24 tunnels; seawater flows through each tunnel and activates a 10 megawatt turbine. Reversible blades drive the dynamos in the turbines through each ebb and flow of the tide, producing electricity. Tidal power is generated by the energy of the sea waves and can average about 90 kilowatts for every 3.3 ft (1 m) of wave length. Rance power station is the world's first fully-operational system and is linked to France's national electric grid. One year after its opening, it was producing 500 megawatts of electricity per annum.

FIRST WIND-POWERED GENERATOR
Denmark 1890

In 1890, Danish scientist P. Lacour devised the first successful wind-powered generator, a windmill using sails and twin fantails on a steel tower. Wind power today is one of the world's fastest-growing energy resources; it is renewable energy and non-polluting (except for visual or aesthetic pollution). Already wind turbines generating a total capacity of over 6000 megawatts have been built and this figure is expected to more than double in the next few years. In Europe alone, wind energy projects produce enough electricity to meet the domestic needs of five million people, and the industry hopes to increase this to 50 million people by 2010.

LARGEST ARTIFICIAL LAKE
Lake Victoria (Victoria Nyanza), Africa
26,418 miles² (68,422 km²)

Lake Victoria borders Kenya, Tanzania and Uganda. It is 210 miles (338 km) long and 150 miles (241 km) at its widest. The level of the natural lake was raised by some three feet (0.91 m) when the Owen Falls Dam was constructed in

An engraving of Lake Victoria in the 1880s. By the 1950s the lake had been dammed, the level rising by 3 ft (1 m) to form the world's largest artificial lake

1954, thus turning it technically into an artificial lake.

LARGEST ARTIFICIAL ISLAND
Flevoland Polders, Netherlands
551 miles² (1427 km²) area

The two Flevoland Polders (land reclaimed from the sea) form a continuous land area and are joined to the rest of the Netherlands by dykes, bridges and causeways. The land was reclaimed during the 1950s and 1960s, and in 1986 the new Dutch province of Flevoland was created. One quarter of Flevoland lies below sea level and the coasts are protected by dykes and sand dunes. If it were not for the dykes, over two-fifths of the land would be almost permanently flooded, and pumps work continually to keep the sea at bay.

LARGEST TIDAL RIVER BARRIER
Oosterschelde Dam, Netherlands
5 miles (8 km)

The Oosterschelde (Eastern Schelde) Dam stretches across the Oosterschelde estuary in the south-west Netherlands. It represents a vital part of the Delta Plan to close the sea inlets of the south-western delta, mainly in the province of Zeeland. This became a matter of national priority after the disastrous gales and spring tides of 1 February 1953 which combined to flood up to 400,000 acres (162,000 hectares) and killed almost 2,000 people. Some 10 dams and two bridges were built between 1960 and 1987, the largest being the Oosterschelde Dam, a storm surge barrier with 61 openings that can be closed when necessary. The openings are generally left open, allowing sea water to flow naturally into the estuary, thus limiting damage to the environment.

BUILDING AND CONSTRUCTION

LARGEST GOVERNMENT OFFICE COMPLEX
Pentagon, Arlington County, Virginia, USA
34 acres (13.77 hectares)
Designed by George Bergstrom, the Pentagon was
constructed in 1941–43. It is made up of five
concentric pentagons or five-sided buildings, with
connecting corridors. Each has five floors plus
mezzanine and basement. The Pentagon is the
headquarters of the United States Defense
departments of the army, navy and air force.

LARGEST COMMERCIAL OFFICE COMPLEX
World Trade Center, New York, USA
12 million ft² (1,116,000 m²) usable floor space
The twin towers of this complex of six buildings
rise to some 1350 ft (411 m) and 110 storeys. The
World Trade Center was built by the New York
and New Jersey Port Authority as a focus for both
government and commercial agencies involved in

international trade. On 26 February 1993, a massive terrorist bomb was detonated in the underground garage, causing several deaths as well as considerable damage to the building.

TALLEST OFFICE BUILDING
Petronas Towers, Kuala Lumpur, Malaysia (1995)
1476 ft (450 m)

TALLEST OFFICE BUILDING IN THE UK
Canary Wharf, London (1990)
800 ft (244 m)

TALLEST OFFICE BUILDING IN NORTH AMERICA
Sears Tower, Chicago, USA (1974)
1453 ft (443 m)

TALLEST MONUMENT
Gateway to the West Arch, St Louis, Missouri, USA
625 ft (190 m)

The arch was designed by Eero Saarinen and erected in 1965 as a celebration of the city's role as a starting point for westward expansion in the 19th century.

LARGEST CATHEDRAL
St John the Divine, New York City, USA
Begun in 1892, this neo-Gothic cathedral has the longest nave in the world.

LARGEST CATHEDRAL IN THE UK
Cathedral Church of Christ, Liverpool, England
This Anglican, neo-Gothic cathedral was begun in

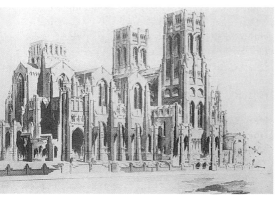

The architect Giles Gilbert Scott's proposed plan for the Cathedral Church of Christ in Liverpool, as shown in the Illustrated London News *of 1903*

1903, but not consecrated until 1978. The central tower rises to some 330 ft (100.6 m).

LARGEST TOMB
Mount Li, near Xi'an, China

Mount Li was discovered by archaeologists in 1974. It is the burial place of Qin Shihuangdi and dates from the Qin (Ch'in) dynasty. Qin Shihuangdi ruled 221–210 BC and first united China, establishing standards for the law, monetary and road systems, weights and measures and written language. The great emperor's body is 'guarded' by 7000 lifesize terracotta warriors, all individually moulded and complete with their crossbows, spears and horses.

HIGHEST CHURCH SPIRE
Ulm Cathedral, Baden-Württemburg, Germany
528 ft (161 m)

This Gothic cathedral was begun in 1377 but not finished until 1890.

HIGHEST CHURCH SPIRE IN THE UK
Salisbury Cathedral, Wiltshire, England
404 ft (123 m)

The cathedral was built in the 13th century and remains one of the finest in Europe.

TALLEST TOWER
KTHI-TV tower, North Dakota, USA
2064 ft (629 m)

TALLEST TOWER IN EUROPE
Ostankino TV tower, Moscow, Russia
1762 ft (537 m)

LONGEST WALL
Great Wall of China
4000 miles (6437 km), including branches
The Great Wall of China was built by Emperor Qin Shihuangdi (*see* **LARGEST TOMB**, *page 135*), in the 3rd century BC to prevent the Huns from attacking and harassing his lands in northern China. It was extended and rebuilt by later Chinese dynasties and stretches from the Yellow Sea to central Asia. The wall is about 30 ft (9 m) high.

LONGEST ARTIFICIAL WATERWAY
Grand Canal, Changzhou-Beijing, China
994 miles (1600 km)
The construction of the Grand Canal is believed to

The Great Wall of China was built in the 3rd century BC and stretches for an astonishing 4000 miles (6437 km)

have begun before the birth of Christ. The northern section was built in the 1200s and the canal is still in use today. The Chinese were the first people to design and build canal locks.

LONGEST ARTIFICIAL WATERWAY IN EUROPE

Volga–Baltic Waterway, Russia
229 miles (368 km)

The Volga–Baltic Waterway runs from Rybinsk to the Gulf of Finland on the Baltic Sea. It is a system of canalized rivers and man-made canals and was completed in 1964.

LONGEST ARTIFICIAL WATERWAY IN NORTH AMERICA

St Lawrence Seaway, Canada/USA
182 miles (293 km)

The St Lawrence seaway was built jointly by the USA and Canada and completed in 1959. Using rivers, lakes and canals, the seaway links the Great Lakes with the Atlantic Ocean.

LONGEST ARTIFICIAL WATERWAY IN SOUTH AMERICA

Panama Canal, Central America
50 miles (80 km)

The Panama Canal cuts across the Isthmus of Panama and links the Atlantic and Pacific oceans. It was constructed by the United States and took ten years and millions of dollars to build. Thousands of labourers forced their way through jungles and swamps, fighting disease and wild animals, to construct the canal, which was completed in 1914.

LONGEST ARTIFICIAL WATERWAY IN AFRICA
Suez Canal, Egypt
100 miles (161 km)

The Suez Canal runs from Port Said, Egypt, to the Gulf of Suez and links the Red Sea and the Mediterranean. It greatly shortens the route for ships between Europe and the Persian Gulf, India, Australia and the Far East. There are no locks in the Suez Canal.

LONGEST ARTIFICIAL WATERWAY IN ASIA
Grand Canal, Changzhou–Beijing, China
994 miles (1600 km)

See LONGEST ARTIFICIAL WATERWAY, *page 136.*

LONGEST BRIDGE
Lake Pontchartrain Causeway (No. 2), USA
23.9 miles (38.5 km)

The twin causeways of Lake Pontchartrain shorten the travelling distance between New Orleans and Mandeville, Louisiana, USA. No. 1 Causeway was completed in 1956 and No. 2 in 1969. Both are made of pre-cast, pre-stressed concrete and are multispan.

Opened in 1869, the Suez Canal linked the Mediterranean and Red seas and is still the longest artificial waterway in Africa. This photograph taken in the 1890s shows shipping at Port Said, the northern entrance to the canal

LONGEST SUSPENSION BRIDGE (MAIN SPAN)
Akashi Kaikyo, Hyogo, Japan
6529 ft (1990 m)

This bridge links Kobe on the island of Honshu to Awaji island and is part of an ongoing project to build 17 bridges which will ultimately connect Honshu to the island of Shikoku.

LONGEST SUSPENSION BRIDGE IN EUROPE (MAIN SPAN)
Store Baelt (Great Belt) Bridge, Denmark (1997)
5905 ft (1800 m)

This is the suspension-bridge element of a huge bridge between Zeeland and Funen which has a total length of 16 miles (26 km).

LONGEST SUSPENSION BRIDGE IN THE UK (MAIN SPAN)
Humber Estuary, Yorkshire/Lincolnshire, England (1981)
5328 ft (1624 m)

LONGEST SUSPENSION BRIDGE IN NORTH AMERICA (MAIN SPAN)
Verrazano Narrows, New York City, USA (1964)
4258 ft (1298 m)

The Verrazano Narrows suspension bridge, the longest in North America, links Brooklyn with Staten Island, and carries twelve lanes of traffic on two separate decks

LONGEST CANTILEVER BRIDGE
Quebec Bridge, Quebec, Canada
Main span 1801 ft (549 m), total length 3238 ft (987 m)

The Quebec Bridge spans the St Laurence River

between Ste Foy and St Nicolas, Quebec. It was completed in 1917.

LONGEST STEEL ARCH BRIDGE
New River Gorge, New River, nr Fayetteville, West Virginia, USA (1977)
Main span 1699 ft (518 m)

LONGEST UNDERSEA TUNNEL
Channel Tunnel, Folkestone, Kent, England to Calais, France (1994)
32$^1/_4$ miles (51.8 km)

LONGEST ROAD TUNNEL
St Gotthard, Göschenen to Airlo, Switzerland (1980)
10 miles (16.1 km)

LONGEST RAILWAY TUNNEL
Seikan Tunnel, linking islands of Honshu and Hokkaido, Japan (1988)
33$^1/_2$ miles (53.8 km)

LONGEST UNDERGROUND RAILWAY TUNNEL
Moscow, Belyaevo to Medvedkovo
19 miles (30.6 km)

WIDEST TUNNEL
Antwerp, Belgium
187 ft (57 m)

The tunnel runs under the River Scheldt; it has eight road and railway lanes, plus routes for cyclists and motorcyclists.

LONGEST WATER TUNNEL
Delaware Aqueduct, New York City, USA
105 miles (168 km)

The water tunnel penetrates to depths as great as 2500 ft (762 m) below ground. It was built between 1937 and 1953.

LARGEST AQUEDUCT SYSTEM
California
685 miles (1102 km)

An aqueduct is a man-made channel designed to carry water to where it is needed. Aqueducts have been constructed since ancient times, although nowadays they have been largely supplanted by waterpipes. The California project has been operational since 1960 and is part of a major plan to redirect water from the northern part of the state as far as the Mexican border, both for domestic and for agricultural uses.

The world's largest railway station is New York's Grand Central Termin

...wn here in a superbly evocative photograph taken by Hal Morey c.1930

LARGEST SPORTS STADIUM
Strahov Stadium, Prague, Czech Republic
240,000 spectators
The Strahov Stadium was built in 1934 for the Sokol gymnastics exhibition.

LARGEST SHOPPING CENTRE
West Edmonton Mall, Alberta, Canada
The West Edmonton Mall offers shoppers over 800 stores, restaurants, hotel, funfair, church, lake, sunbathing and surfing opportunities, zoo and landscaped grounds planted with trees. It was opened in 1981.

LARGEST SHOPPING CENTRE IN EUROPE
MetroCentre, Gateshead, Tyne and Wear, England
The MetroCentre offers over 350 shops, restaurants, cinema and leisure facilities.

LARGEST PORT
Port of New York and New Jersey, New York, USA
751 miles (1208 km) navigable waters
The Port of New York Authority controls all the

waterways and port facilities within 25 miles of the
Statue of Liberty. There are over 250 berths for
large ships and the port handles over 100 million
tons of cargo each year.

BUSIEST PORT
Rotterdam-Europoort, Netherlands
Rotterdam was heavily bombed in World War II
(1939–45) and rebuilding work included a
completely new port. Rotterdam handles millions
of tons of cargo each year, especially oil, petroleum
and grain. Its position at the mouth of the rivers
Meuse and Rhine means that, in addition to large
tankers and other sea-going ships, Rotterdam can
also handle many thousands of cargo-carrying river
barges.

BUSIEST AIRPORT
Heathrow Airport, London, England
54.5 million passengers per annum

LARGEST RAILWAY STATION
Grand Central Terminal, New York City, USA
48 acres (19.4 hectares)
The station was constructed by the American

millionaire Cornelius Vanderbilt (1794–1877) as
the terminal for his Chicago to New York railway
line. The station has 44 platforms.

LARGEST RAILWAY STATION IN THE UK
Waterloo, London
30 acres (12.2 hectares)
Waterloo Station has recently been expanded to
provide facilities for trains using the Channel Tunnel.

FIRST THEME PARK
Disneyland, Anaheim, California, USA (1955)

LARGEST THEME PARK
Disney World, Orlando, Florida, USA (1971)

LARGEST THEME PARK IN EUROPE
Disneyland Paris, Marne-la-Vallée, France (1992)

TRANSPORT

HIGHEST MANNED BALLOON FLIGHT
113,740 ft (34,668 m)

Commander M.D. Ross of the United States Naval
Reserve and his crew broke all records with this
achievement in 1961.

LARGEST AIRSHIP
Hindenburg (LZ129)
804 ft (245 m) long, 134 ft 6 in (41 m) wide

The giant *Hindenburg* was launched on its maiden
flight in 1936. Intended for the transatlantic crossing,
this rigid dirigible balloon filled with hydrogen could
travel at speeds of up to 84 mph (135 km/h),
powered by four 1000 h.p. diesel engines, and could
accommodate around 90 passengers. On 6 May
1937, while docking at Lakehurst, New Jersey, USA,
the *Hindenburg* exploded, killing 35 of its 97
passengers and crew. This terrible accident signalled
the end of commercial airship travel.

LONGEST AIRSHIP FLIGHT
264 hours, March 1957

Led by Commander J.R. Hunt of the United States

The catastrophic end of the Hindenburg, *the world's largest airship, at Lakehurst, New Jersey, USA on 6 May 1937*

Navy, the crew of a ZPG-2 class airship travelled non-stop, via Africa and the Cape Verde islands, from Massachusetts to Florida, USA, without refuelling.

LARGEST PASSENGER AEROPLANE
Boeing 747
Wingspan 211 ft (64.3 m), up to 500 passengers

The 'jumbo jet' needs only two pilots and can fly over 8000 miles (12,874 km) non-stop at a cruise speed of around 403 mph (648.5 km/h). The first 747 flew in 1969. The Boeing company, founded by the American, William E. Boeing (1881–1956), has also been closely involved with the development of the Apollo and Saturn moon rockets and the Minuteman intercontinental ballistic missile.

LARGEST AEROPLANE WINGSPAN
Spruce Goose
319 ft 11 in (97.57 m)

This experimental eight-engined, wooden flying boat made one flight only, piloted by its owner and designer, the American billionaire Howard Hughes. Capable of carrying 700 passengers, this huge machine flew just 0.99 miles (1.6 km) at a height of 69 ft 4 in (21 m). The aircraft is now on display at Long Beach, California.

Two photographs of Chuck Yeager (on the left in the top photograph) taken at Muroc Air Force Base, California on 14 October 1947, the day on which he became the first person to break the sound barrier in air

FIRST MAN TO BREAK THE SOUND BARRIER IN AIR
Charles Yeager

Capt. Charles (Chuck) E. Yeager of the United States Air Force piloted a Bell X-1 rocket plane on 14 October 1947 and became the first man in history to break the sound barrier.

HIGHEST AIR SPEED
2193 mph (3529 km/h)
July 1976

Capt. E.W. Joersz broke all previous records with this flight in a military Lockheed plane known as a Blackbird, a type of plane invisible to radar and therefore ideal for surveillance. The speed of sound (Mach 1) is about 761 mph (1225 km/h) at ground level, but it declines with the increase of altitude.

FASTEST PASSENGER AEROPLANE
Concorde
Cruising speed up to 1304 mph (2100 km/h)

The BAC/Aérospatiale *Concorde*, a joint production between France and the UK, was first flown in 1969 and began regular passenger services in 1976. It is the first and, to date the only, supersonic airliner (i.e. it goes faster than the speed of sound), and has flown between London and New York in as little as three hours. Only 16 *Concordes* have been built.

HIGHEST AEROPLANE FLIGHT
314,750 ft (95,936 m)
In 1962 United States Air Force pilot Major Robert M. White flew his X-15 rocket plane so high that he could qualify as a spaceman! The X-15 is capable of flying at speeds in excess of Mach 5 (five times the speed of sound), making it a hypersonic aircraft.

LARGEST SHIP
Jahre Viking
1504 ft (458 m) long, 226 ft (68.8 m) wide
This supertanker was built in Japan in 1979. Oil tankers carry their cargo over long distances economically and efficiently, but their very size makes them unwieldy and prone to accidents.

LONGEST LINER
Norway
1033 ft (315 m)
The *Norway*, formerly known as the *France*, was

built in France in 1961. She carries around 1000
crew and 2000 passengers.

LARGEST LINER (PASSENGER CAPACITY)
Sovereign of the Seas
2700 passengers

The *Sovereign of the Seas* was built in Norway in
1988 and carries 750 crew.

FASTEST SPEED ON WATER
275 knots (316$\frac{1}{2}$ mph/509 km/h)

The record was set in October 1978 by Ken Warby
in a hydroplane, *The Spirit of Australia*, in New
South Wales, Australia. Hydroplanes, with their
specially-shaped hulls which skim or 'plane' over
the surface of the water, are designed for speed.
The flat or slightly curved bottom of the
hydroplane uses the same principle as the aerofoil,
lifting and keeping the boat on the surface of the
water, and thus allowing it to go faster.

FASTEST ATLANTIC CROSSING
2 days 10 hr 34 min 47 sec

The record was achieved by the crew of the
speedboat *Destriero* in August 1992.

Ken Warby celebrates breaking the world record for the fastest speed on water in his hydroplane The Spirit of Australia

FIRST HOVERCRAFT
SR.NI
The SR.NI hovercraft was designed and built in Britain in 1959, although the idea was first

explored by Sir John Thorneycroft in the 1870s.
Enthusiasm for the hovercraft was high in the
1960s with designers and manufacturers
optimistically envisaging ocean-going hovercraft in
the near future. As it is, Britain is the only country
which uses hovercraft on a commercial scale.
Hovercraft also have military uses.

FASTEST COMMERCIAL HOVERCRAFT
SR.N4
Up to 70 mph (112.7 km/h)
These cross-channel hovercraft, which run between
England and France, are also the largest in regular
commercial use. They can accommodate up to 418
passengers and 60 vehicles.

FIRST NUCLEAR-POWERED PASSENGER SHIP
Savannah
The 593 ft 9 in (181 m) long *Savannah* was built in
the USA in 1959, two years after the world's first
nuclear-powered surface vessel, the Soviet Union
ice-breaker *Lenin*, came into service. The *Savannah*
cruised around the world carrying both passengers
and cargo, but running costs proved to be

prohibitive, and she was taken out of service after only 12 years.

FASTEST STEAM ENGINE
Mallard
125 1/2 mph (202 km/h)
This British streamlined LNER A4 class locomotive achieved the world record in 1938.

FASTEST ELECTRIC TRAIN
L'Atlantique TGV
320 mph (515 km/h)
The French TGV (*Train à Grande Vitesse*, high-speed train), the pride of SNCF railways, still holds the official record (dating from 1991), despite stiff competition, especially from Japan. In December 1997, a prototype manned Japanese maglev (magnetically levitated) train hurtled along on a test run at 332 mph (534.1 km/h).

FASTEST DIESEL ENGINE IN REGULAR SERVICE
Intercity 125
162 mph (261 km/h)
The British Intercity 125 locomotive is certainly

capable of reaching these speeds, but its average speed on the London to Edinburgh run was a slightly less breathtaking 95 mph (153 km/h), before being replaced by electric engines.

FASTEST REGULAR PASSENGER SERVICE
100 mph (160 km/h)
Tokaido line, Japan

The Tokaido line runs between Tokyo and Osaka. The streamlined, electric Hikari trains leave each terminal city four times an hour and complete the 320 mile (515 km) journey in just over three hours.

HIGHEST RAILWAY LINE
Central Railway, Peru
Up to 19,685 ft (6000 m) above sea level

The railway runs between Peru and Bolivia and crosses the Andes mountains. It is used mainly for freight, carrying the minerals which are mined there. The problems of such enormous heights and steep gradients are solved by means of tunnels and toothed rack sections.

HIGHEST RAILWAY STATION
Condor, Bolivia
15,705 ft (4787 m)

LONGEST RAIL JOURNEY
Moscow to Vladivostok, Russia
5786 miles (9311 km), approx 8 days
The Trans-Siberian railway was begun in 1891, but not finished until 1915. Russia has the highest passenger railway usage in Europe.

LONGEST STRETCH OF STRAIGHT RAIL TRACK
Nullarbor Plain, Western Australia
296 $^3/_4$ miles (478 km)
This track forms part of the railway line which stretches across Australia from Perth on the west to Sydney on the east. The journey, on the *Indian Pacific* train, is a total of 2445 $^1/_2$ miles (3938 km) and lasts for three days.

FIRST UNDERGROUND SYSTEM
London Underground
The first underground trains ran between Paddington and Farringdon stations in 1863 and

used coal-burning steam engines. The air extraction system failed to keep the tunnels clean, but despite the fumes the system proved popular. Other cities followed suit, including Glasgow, Budapest, Paris and New York. The underground in Moscow was begun in 1932 and carries around 6.5 million passengers each day, more than any other system.

LONGEST PRODUCTION CAR
Bugatti Type 41 (Golden Bugatti or La Royale)
22 ft (6.7 m)

Ettore Bugatti (1881–1947) was born in Milan, Italy. He began to build luxury and racing cars in Alsace in 1909, and in the 1920s produced the Royale, probably one of the most luxurious and meticulously-constructed cars of all time. It was certainly one of the most expensive and only a handful (6–8) were ever completed.

BEST-SELLING PRODUCTION CAR
Volkswagen Beetle
Over 21 million sold

The Volkswagen ('people's car') company was founded in 1937 by the German government to produce a low-priced car for ordinary people. The car was first named the Beetle, because of its distinctive, rounded appearance, by an American advertising company. The design remained virtually the same until production ceased in the mid-1990s; however, a newer, more up-to-date model has now been developed.

FASTEST SPEED ON LAND
763 mph (1228 km/h)

Andy Green, a British airforce pilot, achieved this record on 15 October 1997 in Black Rock Desert, Nevada, USA. Green actually broke the sound barrier twice in his jet car, *Thrust SSC*, averaging 763 mph (1228 km/h), which was above the speed of sound under local conditions. The first run was made two days earlier, but was not officially recognized because Green failed to complete two separate runs within an hour as required – he took 61 minutes to complete his two runs. The second attempt, on 15 October, puts him in the record books for a feat which many people thought could never be achieved.

FASTEST PRODUCTION CAR
Lamborghini Diablo SV
190+ mph (305.8+ km/h)

On 25 September 1980 Richard Noble broke the British land speed record in Thrust 2. *This car, photographed at RAF Greenham Common, was the forerunner to Noble's* Thrust SSC, *driven by Andy Green, which went on the break the record for the fastest speed on land on 15 October 1997*

The Lamborghini Diablo accelerates from 0–60 mph (0–96.56 km/h) in 3.8 seconds and costs around £136,000.

FASTEST PRODUCTION MOTORBIKE
V & M Honda Blackbird
200 mph (322 km/h)

LARGEST BICYCLE
Frankencycle
73 ft (22.24 m) long, 10 ft (3.05 m) wheel diameter
The *Frankencycle* was built in California in 1988 and ridden by four men for a distance of 807 ft (246 m).

COUNTRY WITH HIGHEST NUMBER OF BICYCLES
China
300 million (estimated)

HIGHEST ROAD
18,000 ft (5486.4 m) above sea level
This road lies on the borders of Tibet and China in the Himalayas.

LOWEST ROAD
1290 ft (393 m) below sea level
The road runs along the shores of the Dead Sea in Israel.

LONGEST ROAD
Pan-American Highway
30,000 miles (48,000 km) total length

The Pan-American Highway runs from Alaska to
Chile, with connecting routes extending to
Paraguay, Argentina and Brazil. The road links the
east and west coasts of South America and includes
the capitals of 17 countries along the way. It was
originally designed to be a single highway, but it
now includes many feeder routes, which connect it
to previously remote and isolated places. Once out
of the United States, the landscape varies from
dense jungles to remote mountains, and the
spectacular scenery is home to all kinds of
wildlife.

COUNTRY WITH THE DENSEST NETWORK
OF ROADS
Belgium
**Approx 2600 miles (4200 km) of road to every
621 miles^2 (1000 km^2) of land.**

WIDEST STREET
426 ft (130 m)
Avenida 9 de Julio, Buenos Aires, Argentina

BIGGEST CITY SQUARE
Tiananmen Square, Beijing, China
100 acres (40.5 hectares)

The square was originally laid in 1651 and
subsequently enlarged several times. Its name is
derived from the Tiananmen gate (Gate of
Heavenly Peace), which led into the former
Imperial Palace at one end of the square. In June
1989, a massive pro-democracy student demon-
stration in the square was forcibly put down by the
army. Estimates of the number killed by troops
range from several hundred to many thousands,
and the true figure will probably never be known.
Subsequently, Tiananmen Square has become a
symbol of Chinese Communist repression.

ARTS AND ENTERTAINMENT

FIRST SOUND FILM
The Jazz Singer (1927)

The film was not a sound film as it is generally understood today, but included some scenes with Al Jolson, the star, singing and speaking with synchronized sound. The sound was recorded on a disc, then synchronized with the film strip. This cumbersome system was soon replaced by an electronic system which recorded sound directly on to the film strip. *The Jazz Singer* was, however, a major breakthrough in film, although some film experts and critics predicted that sound 'would never catch on' with the film-going public!

FIRST FULL-LENGTH ANIMATED FEATURE FILM
Snow White and the Seven Dwarfs (1937)

Animated cartoons need 24 separate pictures to represent just one second of screen movement, and *Snow White* is estimated to contain over 450,000 individual drawings. The film was shown all over the world, and dubbed into 13 languages.

LARGEST FILM SET
55 acres (22 hectares)
The Roman forum in *The Fall of the Roman Empire* (USA, 1964).

MOST EXTRAS
300,000 *Gandhi* (GB, 1982)

MOST EXPENSIVE FILM
***Titanic* (USA, 1997) £200 million**

GREATEST PROFIT MADE FROM ONE FILM
***Titanic* (USA, 1997) £68 million**

GREATEST LOSS MADE FROM ONE FILM
***Cutthroat Island* (USA, 1995) £53 million**

COUNTRY WITH LARGEST FILM OUTPUT
India
The Indian film industry produces around 750 films a year.

EUROPEAN COUNTRY WITH LARGEST FILM OUTPUT
France

The French film industry produces around 140 films a year.

FIRST OSCAR AWARDS
1928

The 'Oscars' are awarded by the Academy of Motion Picture Arts and Sciences, which initiated the awards in 1927 to improve the quality and prestige of film-making. The Oscar statuette is a gold-plated, nude, male figure standing on a reel of film punched with five holes, each representing a branch of film-making. Legend has it that a librarian at the Academy commented that the statuette looked like her Uncle Oscar and so it was named.

FILM WITH MOST OSCAR AWARDS
11 *Ben Hur* (USA, 1959), *Titanic* (USA, 1997)

FILM WITH MOST OSCAR NOMINATIONS
14 *All About Eve* (USA, 1950), *Titanic* (USA, 1997)

MOST OSCAR AWARDS
29 Walt Disney Studios

MOST OSCAR-NOMINATED ACTOR NEVER TO WIN AN AWARD
7 Richard Burton

MOST BEST ACTRESS AWARDS
4 Katharine Hepburn

MOST BEST ACTOR AWARDS
2 Spencer Tracy, Fredric March, Gary Cooper, Marlon Brando, Dustin Hoffmann, Tom Hanks, Jack Nicholson

LONGEST THEATRICAL RUN
The Mousetrap

Agatha Christie's *The Mousetrap* opened at the Ambassadors Theatre in London on 25 November 1952. The play transferred to St Martin's Theatre and is still running, having now achieved over 19,250 performances.

SHORTEST PLAY
35 seconds
Breath by Samuel Beckett

LONGEST-RUNNING MUSICAL
Cats

Katharine Hepburn has been awarded the best actress Oscar a record four times, for her performances in Morning Glory *(1933),* Guess Who's Coming to Dinner? *(1967),* The Lion in Winter *(1968) and* On Golden Pond *(1981).*

Andrew Lloyd-Webber's *Cats* is based on T.S. Eliot's poems from his *Old Possum's Book of Practical Cats*. In September 1991, Andrew Lloyd-Webber became the first person in musical history to have six shows running simultaneously in London's West End.

FASTEST-SELLING SINGLE
Candle in the Wind (1997) Elton John
The 1997 version of *Candle in the Wind*, written by Elton John and Bernie Taupin, is a reworking of their earlier tribute to film star Marilyn Monroe, now dedicated to Diana, Princess of Wales. The record sold over 600,000 copies on its day of release, 13 September 1997.

BIGGEST-SELLING SINGLE
Candle in the Wind (1997)
Over 31 million copies were sold worldwide in one month. The previous holder of this record was the 1942 Bing Crosby version of Irving Berlin's *White Christmas*, which has sold a total of 30 million copies worldwide. See **FASTEST-SELLING SINGLE**, *above*.

BIGGEST-SELLING SINGLE IN THE UK

See BIGGEST-SELLING SINGLE, *page 174.*

FIRST SINGLE TO SELL OVER 2 MILLION IN THE UK

Mull of Kintyre (1977) **Paul McCartney and Wings**

BIGGEST-SELLING ALBUM

Thriller (1982) **Michael Jackson 45 million copies**

BIGGEST-SELLING SOLO SINGER
Elvis Presley

Presley (1935–77) had 14 consecutive million-selling hits and sold some 500 million records during his lifetime. Over 20 million records were sold in the 24 hours after his death. He was the most successful recording artist ever known.

BIGGEST-SELLING UK SOLO SINGER
Elton John

Elton John, born Reginald Dwight in 1947, with his songwriting partner, Bernie Taupin, has enjoyed over 25 years of success, with hit songs every year in both the UK and USA.

MOST SUCCESSFUL GROUP
The Beatles

The Beatles (John Lennon, Paul McCartney, Ringo Starr and George Harrison) were part of the 1960s 'Merseybeat' sound from Liverpool. The group dominated pop music during the sixties and soon achieved international fame. The Beatles were

Worldwide sales of The Beatles' records are reckoned to be more than a billion, making the group the most successful ever. This November 1963 photograph shows John, Paul, George and Ringo appearing on The Ken Dodd Show

awarded 47 gold discs, and their total record sales worldwide are estimated to be more than a billion.

MOST NUMBER 1 SINGLES
17 Elvis Presley, The Beatles

LARGEST SCULPTURE
Stone Mountain heads, Georgia, USA

The faces of the American Civil War Confederate generals Robert E. Lee and Stonewall Jackson, together with that of the Confederate president, Jefferson Davis, are carved over 800 ft (245 m) high on the side of Stone Mountain, near Decatur, Georgia. The huge faces are over 90 ft (27 m) in length and the carving took over eight years to complete, from 1963 to 1972.

LARGEST SCULPTURE IN THE UK
***Angel of the North*, near Gateshead, England**

The *Angel of the North* stands on a windswept hillside beside the A1 road and the main east coast railway line. It measures 65 ft (19.8 m) in height and has a 175 ft (53.3 m) wingspan. The artist is Anthony Gormley and the sculpture cost £800,000. Built to withstand 100 mph (160 km/h) winds, the *Angel* contains some

200 tons (203 tonnes) of steel, each wing weighs 50 tons (50.8 tonnes) and is held in place by 88 bolts.

MOST FAMOUS STATUE
Statue of Liberty, New York Harbour, USA

The statue's full name is *Liberty Enlightening the World* and it was gifted to the USA in 1886 by France, as a symbol of friendship between the two countries. The statue is 302 ft (92 m) high and represents a female figure with a torch in her right hand and a tablet, inscribed 4 July 1776 (the date of the Declaration of American Independence), in her left hand.

MOST FAMOUS PAINTING
Mona Lisa

Leonardo da Vinci (1452–1519) painted the *Mona Lisa* in around 1504. It is now on show in the Louvre Museum, Paris, where it is heavily guarded. Its value is impossible to assess.

HIGHEST PRICE PAID FOR A PAINTING
$82 million (£49 million)

Paid in 1990 for *Dr Gachet*, a portrait by Vincent van Gogh (1853–90).

The Statue of Liberty in New York Harbour is the world's most famous statue. This engraving from the Illustrated London News *shows the statue's inauguration in 1886*

LONGEST OPERA
Die Meistersinger von Nürnberg
5 hours

The Mastersingers of Nuremberg was composed by Richard Wagner (1813–83), who also wrote the longest opera cycle, the 15-hour *Ring of the Nibelung*.

LARGEST ORCHESTRAL SCORE
Gothic Symphony

Havergal Brian (1876–1972) wrote this work for an orchestra of some 200 performers and choirs of 400–600 singers.

QUIETEST MUSICAL PERFORMANCE
4 Minutes 33 Seconds

John Cage (1912–92) was a pupil of Schoenberg. His music reveals a passion for experimentation and innovation, and his belief that all sounds are, in fact, musical sounds is manifested in *4 Minutes 33 Seconds*, in which the performers and audience sit in complete silence, aware only of the sounds around them.

LONGEST-RUNNING TELEVISION DRAMA PRODUCTION
Coronation Street
9 December 1960 to present

LONGEST-SERVING TELEVISION PRESENTER ON ONE PROGRAMME
Patrick Moore *The Sky at Night*
1957 to present

HIGHEST-SELLING WRITER (FICTION)
Agatha Christie

Agatha Christie (1890–1976) began writing while working as a nurse in World War I (1914–18). Her first novel, *The Mysterious Affair at Styles* (1920), introduced the Belgian detective, Hercule Poirot, to the world. Jane Marple, the spinsterish amateur sleuth, first appeared in 1930 in *Murder at the Vicarage*. Agatha Christie's play, *The Mousetrap*, is the longest-running play ever known (*see* **LONGEST THEATRICAL RUN**, page 172). Her books have been translated into 44 languages and are estimated to have sold over 2 billion copies worldwide.

HIGHEST-SELLING LIVING WRITER (FICTION)
Barbara Cartland

Barbara Cartland (born 1901) has written over 600 books and still produces some 23 new titles each year. She writes only romantic fiction and has an estimated 600 million readers worldwide.

HIGHEST-SELLING BOOK
The Bible

Precise figures are impossible to give, but the Bible is

AGATHA CHRISTIE

Dame Agatha Christie is the world's highest-selling fiction writer.
This stylised portrait by Butterfield appeared in The Courier *of*
December 1949

thought to have sold over five billion copies worldwide; it has been translated into 350 languages.

OLDEST NATIONAL DAILY NEWSPAPER IN THE UK
The Times, founded 1788

DAILY NEWSPAPER WITH HIGHEST NUMBER OF UK READERS
The Sun, founded 1969, over 4 million readers

SUNDAY NEWSPAPER WITH HIGHEST NUMBER OF UK READERS
News of the World, founded 1843, over 4 million readers

OLDEST ANNUAL PUBLICATION IN THE UK
Old Moore's Almanac, founded 1700

Dr Moore called his almanac *Vox Stellarum* or 'Voice of the Stars', and it is dedicated to astrological predictions and forecasts for the coming year.

Sport

MOST OLYMPIC PARTICIPANTS
10,700 accredited athletes, Atlanta, Georgia, USA (1996)
The XXVI Olympiad which ran from 19 July to 4 August 1996 in Atlanta had the largest number of participants ever recorded, one third of them women. Every invited National Olympic Committee sent a team, a total of 197 teams, the first time in history that this has happened.

MOST GOLD MEDALS IN SUMMER OLYMPICS
Men: 10 Raymond Ewry, USA (track and field)
Women: 9 Larissa Latynina, USSR (gymnastics)

MOST GOLD MEDALS IN ONE SUMMER OLYMPICS
Men: 7 Mark Spitz, USA, 1972 (swimming)
Women: 6 Kristin Otto, GDR, 1988 (swimming)

MOST MEDALS IN SUMMER OLYMPICS
Men: 15 Nikolai Andrianov, USSR (gymnastics)
Women: 18 Larissa Latynina, USSR (gymnastics)

Mark Spitz won seven gold medals for swimming at the 1972 Munich Olympics. Each gold medal was won in a record-breaking time

TRACK AND FIELD (MEN)

100 m Maurice Greene, USA 9.79 sec (1999)

200 m Michael Duane Johnson, USA 19.32 sec (1996)

400 m Michael Johnson, USA 43.18 sec (1999)

800 m Wilson Kipketer, Denmark, 1.41.11 (1997)

1500 m Hitcham El Guerrouj, Morocco, 3.26.00 (1998)

Marathon Belayneh Dinsamo, Ethiopia 2.06.50 (1988)

High jump Javier Sotomayor, Cuba 8 ft ¹/₂ in (2.46 m) (1993)

Long jump Mike Powell, USA 29 ft 4¹/₂ in (8.95 m) (1991)

Javelin Jan Zelezny, Czech Republic 323 ft 1 in (98.48 m) (1996)

TRACK AND FIELD (WOMEN)

100 m Florence Griffith Joyner, USA 10.49 sec (1988)

200 m Florence Griffith Joyner, USA 21.34 sec (1988)

400 m Marita Koch, GDR 47.60 sec (1985)

800 m Jarmila Kratochvilov, Czechoslovakia 1.53.28 (1983)

1500 m Qu Yunxia, China 3.50.46 (1993)

Marathon Tegla Loraipe, Kenya 2.20.07 (1998)

High jump Stefka Kostadinova, Bulgaria 6 ft 10$^1/_4$ in (2.09 m) (1987)

Long jump Galina Chistakova, USSR 24 ft 8$^1/_4$ in (7.52 m) (1988)

Javelin Petra Felke, GDR 262 ft 5 in (79.98 m) (1988)

FOOTBALL

**First World Cup winner
Uruguay, 1930**

**Most World Cup wins
4 Brazil**

RUGBY

**Most Rugby Union 5 Nations Championship wins (post-war)
11 England**

**Most Grand Slam wins (winning all four matches)
11 England**

**Triple Crown wins
20 England**

CRICKET

FIRST TEST MATCH
15 March 1877, England v. Australia (London)
Australia won by 15 runs

NARROWEST VICTORY IN A TEST MATCH
1 run
Australia beat India, Madras, 1987–8
Australia beat India, Brisbane, 1992

HIGHEST INNINGS TOTAL IN A TEST MATCH
903 for 7 wickets
Declared by England against Australia, August 1938, London

LOWEST INNINGS TOTAL IN A TEST MATCH
26
Scored by New Zealand against England, 1955, Auckland

TENNIS

Most men's Wimbledon titles
13 Hugh 'Laurie' Doherty, GB

Most women's Wimbledon titles
20 Billie-Jean King, USA

Most men's Wimbledon singles titles
6 Pete Sampras, USA

Most women's Wimbledon singles titles
9 Martina Navratilova, USA

Martina Navratilova has won the Wimbledon singles title a record-breaking nine times, the last time in 1990. She is shown here celebrating her eighth win in 1987

Index

Σ Aurigae 38
4 Minutes 33 Seconds 180

Aconcagua 9
African elephant 56–57
African goliath beetle 85
Aldrin, Edward 'Buzz' 47
All About Eve 171
Alpha Centauri 38
Amazon 19
Angel Falls 20
Angel of the North 177
Arabian Sea 23
Arctic giant 77
Arecibo, Puerto Rico 43
Arica, Chile 27
Armstrong, Neil 46–47
Asiatic elephant 61
Astor, Viscountess (Nancy) 114
Atacama Desert 27
Avenida 9 de Julio, Buenos Aires 167

Bandaranaike, Sirimavo 113
Bee hummingbird 69, 75
Ben Hur 171
Ben Nevis 8–9
Black mamba 80
Blue whale 55
Boeing 747 153
Bombay 100
Braemar 26
Bratsk 127
Brazilian brachycephalids 79
Brazilian huntsman 83
Bristlecone pine 50
Brotulids 76
Brúarjökull Glacier 22
Buenos Aires 99
Bugatti Type 41 163

Burton, Richard 172
Buttle, Elizabeth 105

Cairngorm 28
Cairo 100
Calment, Jeanne Louise 105
Canary Wharf 133
Candle in the Wind 174
Cane toad 78
Cartland, Barbara 181
Caspian Sea 12
Cathedral Church of Christ, Liverpool 134
Cats 172
Central Railway, Peru 161
Ceres 39
Channel Tunnel 144
Cheetah 58–59
Cheltenham 25
Cherrapunji, India 26
Chihuahua 66–67
Christie, Agatha 172, 181–82
Chutes de Khone 21
Cilaos, Isle de Réunion 26
Clydesdale/Shire 65
Coast redwood 49
Coco de mer 51
Collins, Michael 47
Common cold 107
Common silver fir 49
Common toad 79
Concorde 155
Condor, Bolivia 162
Coronation Street 180
Cotopaxi, Ecuador 32
Creutzfeldt-Jacob Disease 107
Cullinan Diamond 87–88
Cumulonimbus 27
Cutthroat Island 170

Dalla Corta, Rosanna 105

Dalol, Ethiopia 26
Death cap 55
Delaware Aqueduct 145
Devlin, Bernadette 115
Die Meistersinger von Nürnberg 179
Disney 150, 171
Dog Star 39

Ease Gill 11
Emperor (imperial) scorpion 83
Emperor penguin 72–73
Entada scandens 51

Falabella 65
Fat-tailed scorpion 84
Feather-winged beetles 85
Ffynnon Dhu 12
Flevoland Polders 130
Fort Keogh, Montana, USA 29
Frankencycle 166

Galileo 40
Gandhi 170
Gargarin, Yuri 44–45
Gates, Bill 118
Gateway to the West Arch 133
General Sherman Tree 49
Giant redwood or giant sequoia 49
Gigantic waterlily 52
Giraffe 56
Goliath bird-eating spider 82
Goliath frog 79
Gopalganj, Bangladesh 28
Gore-Booth, Constance 115
Gorilla 72
Gothic Symphony 180
Grand Canal,

Changzhou-Beijing 136, 139
Grand Canyon 15–16
Grand Central Terminal 146, 149
Great Man-Made River Project 128
Great Wall of China 136–37
Green, Andy 164

Hawaiian Islands 10–11
Heathrow Airport 149
Helium 121
Hepburn, Katharine 172–73
Hillary, Edmund 7–8
Hindenburg 151–52
Hoary marmot 64
Holtermann Nugget 91
Hope Pearl 90
Hubble Space Telescope 44
Humber Estuary 142
Hummingbirds 71, 74
Humpback whale 61
Hungary 106
Hurricane Andrew 35
Hydrogen 119

Indian elephant 64
Intercity 125 160
Irish wolfhound 66

Jahre Viking 156
Jean Bernard 11
Jenkinson, Robert Banks 113
Jodrell Bank Experimental Station 41–42
John, Elton 175
Jupiter 36

Keck telescope 40
Ken Warby 157–58
Kilimanjaro 10

Kitti's hog-nosed bat 56
Koikoi (poison-arrow frog) 79
Komodo dragon 81
Kondakova, Yelena 48
Kori (giant) bustard 69
Krakatoa 29, 31
Krásnohorská Cave 12
KTHI-TV tower 136

L'Atlantique TGV 160
Lake Baikal 15
Lake Pontchartrain Causeway (No. 2) 139
Lake Superior 15
Lake Victoria 129–30
Lambert Glacier 21
Lamborghini Diablo SV 164
Lesser mouse lemur 63
Lithium 122
Loch Lomond 13
Loch Ness 14–15
London 99, 162
Louis XIV 109

Mackenzie-Peace 18
Maidenhair tree 50
Maine Coon, Ragdoll 66
Mallard 160
Mallee fowl 73
Mammoth Cave 11
Mariana Trench 23
Marshall Islands 96
Martinstown 27
Mastiff 66
Mayfly 85
McCaughey 105
MetroCentre 148
Mexico City 98–99
Microbothus pusillus 84
Mohammed, Gul 102
Mona Lisa 178
Mont Blanc 8
Moore, Patrick 180

Mount Everest pika 61
Mount Li 135
Mt Cook 10
Mt Etna 32
Mt Everest 7, 10
Mt McKinley 8
Mt Pelée 30
Mt Washington Observatory, New Hampshire 28
Mull of Kintyre 175
Murray 20
Myotis lucifugus 56

Navratilova, Martina 189
Neutron stars 38
New River Gorge 144
News of the World 183
Newton, Isaac 39
Nile 18–19
Noble, Richard 165
Nullarbor Plain 162

Old Moore's Almanac 183
Oosterschelde Dam 131
Orb-weaving spiders 82
Ord 29
Osmium 122
Ostankino TV tower 136
Ostrich 68, 75
Owen Falls 127

Pacific Ocean 22–23
Pan-American Highway 167
Panama Canal 138
Panther Opal 91
Paris 98
Patu marplesi 82
Pentagon 132
Perceval, Spencer 113
Peregrine falcon 71
Petronas Towers 133
Pioneer 10 44

Pitt, William, the Younger 112, 115, 117
Platystele stenostachya 51
Pluto 36–37
Poll an Ionana 12
Polyakov, Valery 48
Presley, Elvis 175
Pronghorn antelope 59
Puffball 54
Pygmy goby 76

Quebec Bridge 143

Rafflesia 53
Rance 128
Reticulated python 80
Rinks Isbrae 22
Rogun 126
Rotterdam-Europoort 149
Ruppell's vulture 72

Saguaro 54
Sahara 22
Salisbury Cathedral 135
Sarawak Chamber 12
Savannah 159
Sea coconut 51
Sea snake 81
Sears Tower 133
Seawasps 77
Seikan Tunnel 144
Sequoia National Park 50
Severn 19
Sharman, Helen 48
Sherpa Tensing 7
Siberian crane 68
Singapura 67
Sirius 39
Smallpox 107
Snow White and the Seven Dwarfs 169
Sovereign of the Seas 157
Sperm whale 62

Spitz, Mark 184–85
Spotted octopus 78
Sprinkling Tarn 27
Spruce Goose 153
St Gotthard 144
St John the Divine 134
St Lawrence Seaway 138
Statue of Liberty 178–79
Stick insects 84
Stone Mountain heads 177
Store Baelt (Great Belt) Bridge 142
Strahov Stadium 148
Suez Canal 139–40
Swifts 71
Sydney 100

Taipan 81
Tangshan 34
Tensing Norgay 8
Tereshkova, Valentina Vladimirovna 47
Thatcher, Margaret 114
The Beatles 176
The Bible 181
The Jazz Singer 169
The Mousetrap 172, 181
The Spirit of Australia 157–58
The Sun 183
The Times 183
Three-toed sloth 60
Thriller 175
Thrust SSC 164–65
Tiananmen Square, Beijing 168
Titanic 170–71
Trans-Alaskan pipeline 125
Trans-Siberian pipeline 126
Transuranic elements 120
Tuberculosis 108

Tungsten 121
Turukhansk 127

Ulm Cathedral 135
Unionville, Maryland 26
Uranium 120
Uranus 37
Urengoy 126
Utigardsfossen Falls 20

V & M Honda Blackbird 166
Venus 36
Verrazano Narrows 142–43
Victoria 110–11
Virginia (Common) opossum 54
VLA, Socorro, New Mexico 43
Volga 18
Volga–Baltic Waterway 137
Volkswagen Beetle 163
Vostok Base, Antarctica 25

Wadlow, Robert Pershing 102–03
Walpole, Robert 112
Wandering albatross 70
Water 104
Waterloo 150
Watermeal 52
Weever fish 76
Welcome Stranger 91
West Edmonton Mall 148
Whale shark 75
World Trade Center 132

Yangtze 19
Yeager, Charles 154–55
Yellowstone National Park 33
Yerkes Observatory 40

COLLINS GEM
BABIES'
names
a ? z
a mine of information

COLLINS GEM
BEER
a mine of information

COLLINS GEM
BIRDS
a mine of information

COLLINS GEM
CALORIE
Counter

COLLINS GEM
FACT FILE
a mine of information

COLLINS GEM
FENG SHUI
a mine of information

COLLINS GEM
F.LAGS
a mine of information

COLLINS GEM
Healthy
EATING
a mine of information

COLLINS GEM
QUOTATIONS
a mine of information

COLLINS GEM
SAS
Self-Defence
a mine of information

COLLINS GEM
SAS
Survival Guide
a mine of information

COLLINS GEM
SEASHORE

COLLINS GEM
TREES
a mine of information

COLLINS GEM
Understanding
DREAMS
a mine of information

COLLINS GEM
WILD
flowers
a mine of information

COLLINS GEM
WINE
Dictionary